W9-CAN-020

For Adam and all children
who love adventure
KH

To Vitti with love
HC

Text copyright © 1990 by Katharine Holabird
Illustrations copyright © 1990 by Helen Craig

All rights reserved. No part of this book may be reproduced or transmitted in any form or by any means, electronic or mechanical, including photocopying, recording, or by any information storage and retrieval system, without permission in writing from the publisher.

Published by Clarkson N. Potter, Inc., a Random House company,
201 East 50th Street, New York, New York 10022

Originally published in Great Britain by ABC in 1990

CLARKSON POTTER, POTTER, and colophon are trademarks of Clarkson N. Potter, Inc.

Printed and bound in Hong Kong by Imago Services (HK) Ltd.

Library of Congress Cataloging-in-Publication Data
Holabird, Katharine.
    Alexander and the magic boat / [Katharine Holabird,
illustrated by Helen Craig].
        p.   cm.
    Summary: Alexander, a little boy with a big imagination,
takes his mother on a voyage in his magic boat.
    ISBN 0-517-58142-6 $11.95
    [1. Imagination — Fiction.   2. Mothers and sons — Fiction.]
I. Craig, Helen, ill.   II. Title.
PZ7.H689Aj 1990
[E] — dc20   90-7252
                                                                  CIP

ISBN 0-517-58142-6
ISBN 0-517-58149-3 (GLB edition)

10 9 8 7 6 5 4 3 2 1

First American edition

Alexander
and the Magic Boat

Story by Katharine Holabird   Illustrations by Helen Craig

Clarkson N. Potter, Inc./Publishers NEW YORK

Alexander loved to imagine great adventures, and every day he thought up something new.

One day, his mother gave him a real captain's hat, and Alexander decided to become a fearless captain of the high seas. He made a boat out of two armchairs, and sailed off to explore faraway places. But it got lonely sailing the seven seas, and he wished that someone would come with him.

He wanted to invite his mother, but she was always very busy. Alexander's mother could do a million things, and Alexander wished that he could do everything as easily as she did. She could cook, climb trees, stand on her head and she could bandage bleeding knees very gently.

She could fix bicycles and she could glue broken toys back together. She knew all about computers and microscopes, and she loved singing operas in the shower. Best of all, Alexander's mother wasn't afraid of spiders, and if she found one she gave it to Alexander to keep in a jar.

Alexander wished that he could give his mother something special, too, even though she always said that his hugs and kisses were the best presents in the world.

Then one afternoon, Alexander's mother stopped working and sat down. "I've been busy all day," she said. "I think I'll just rest for a minute."

Alexander looked at his mother in surprise. Then he had an idea.

"You can rest on my magic boat," Alexander suggested. "I'll be the captain and take you across the sea."

Alexander put on his cap and pushed the two armchairs together
again. He brought some peanut butter and bread, in case they got
hungry, and took his spider for good luck.

His mother smiled and put up her feet, while Alexander jumped
to the deck to steer. Then off they sailed together, across the
deep blue sea.

"This is a magic boat," Alexander explained. "It can take you anywhere. Where would you like to go?"

Alexander's mother thought for a moment. "I always wanted to see the other side of the world," she said.

"Let's go!" shouted Alexander, as the magic boat sailed across the sparkling water.

They travelled past dancing dolphins and
singing whales, past schools of flying fish and
families of smiling seals. Alexander and his
mother sang an opera with the whales. They
splashed with the dolphins. They reached
out to tickle two enormous green turtles
that swam slowly by, while the magic boat
sailed on and on, following the song of the
sea all the way to the other side of the world.

"I think I see an island!" Alexander pointed in the distance. "Let's explore," said his mother, shading her eyes.

No sooner had Alexander landed his boat than three greedy pirates leaped out of the shadows. "AH-HA! A perfect boat for pirates!" They grabbed Alexander and his mother.

"Help!" called Alexander's mother, kicking one of the pirates on the shin bone.

"OOOH!" shouted the pirate, hopping on one leg.

Then Alexander took his spider out of the jar and wiggled it under the pirates' noses.

"EEEEK!" shrieked the pirates, who were terrified of spiders.

"Please don't let that horrible spider touch us!" they cried, falling to their knees. The pirates begged for mercy and promised to be good.

"We've been shipwrecked here—our boat has a terrible leak!" they wailed.

"My mother can fix it," said Alexander proudly, and his mother borrowed a hammer and banged their boat back together before they could say "Captain Hook!". Then Alexander made them all peanut butter sandwiches and the pirates swore they would be best friends forever.

When they had finished eating, the pirates clambered aboard their pirate ship and waved goodbye.

Then Alexander and his mother spent the afternoon digging for buried treasure. Alexander presented his mother with an old silver spoon and a long-lost key. They didn't even notice that the sky was turning dark and the sea was getting rough.

"A hurricane!" cried Alexander. "If the boat blows away, we'll never get back!"

The magic boat was bucking and leaping in the foam, and Alexander caught the rope just before it broke away.

He jumped on board with his mother and the boat plunged into the storm.

Then Alexander steered the magic boat back through waves that
were higher than houses and winds that whistled and roared.
Thunder and lightning exploded in the sky, and the dolphins,
seals and whales hid in the wild darkness of the sea.

But Alexander was
such a good captain
that his mother fell fast asleep until they were safely home again.

Alexander carefully tied up his magic boat before he climbed into his mother's lap.

His mother stretched and smiled. "Thank you for the trip to the other side of the world," she said. "You know a lot about the sea, and pirates too! Will you take me on your boat again?"

"Yes! But I still have one more present for you," smiled Alexander, and he gave his mother a very special hug and kiss.

Ogre
(Giant)

Troll

Goblin

Mermaid
(Merrow)

Griffin

Peryton

W9-BKO-095

For Liz

Text copyright © 1998 Rhett Ransom Pennell.
Illustrations © 1998 by Rhett Ransom Pennell.
Typography by Alicia Mikles.
All rights reserved including the right of reproduction
in whole or in part in any form. Printed in China.
For information address: Greene Bark Press
PO Box 1108 Bridgeport, CT 06601-1108
Second Printing

Publisher's Catalog-in-Publication
(Provided by Quality Books Inc.,)
Pennell, Rhett Ransom.
Excuse Me, Are You A Dragon? / by Rhett Ransom Pennell.

p. cm.
Preassigned LCCN:98-71909
ISBN: 1-880851-34-2
SUMMARY: A young king thinks it would be fun to have a dragon to
fight, so he sends a knight to find one and bring it back to the kingdom.

1. Dragons--Juvenile fiction. 2. Animals, Mythical--Juvenile fiction.
3. Knights and knighthood--Juvenile fiction. I.Title.

PZ7.P38465Ex 1998   [E]
                           QB198-11025

Excuse Me, Are You A Dragon?

Excuse Me, Are You A Dragon?

BY RHETT RANSOM PENNELL

Greene Bark Press

"A dragon!!" yelled young King Edwin. "That's what this kingdom needs. A big, scary dragon!"

It was way past the king's bedtime. He had eaten too many royal cookies that night. Cookies always made him bouncy and gave him strange ideas.

"But your Majesty," protested Sir Gordon, the king's uncle and commander of the royal knights, "Your kingdom is wonderful just as it is. What would we do with a dragon?"

"We would fight it!" said the king. "We would protect people from its dreadful dragon claws and from its fiery dragon breath. Having a dragon around would be such fun!"

Sir Gordon didn't think it sounded like fun at all.

"Uncle Gordon," proclaimed King Edwin, "I command you to find a dragon who will attack my kingdom."

He was king that meant he got to boss his relatives around.

The next morning, Sir Gordon mounted Sturdy Roger, his best horse, and rode off in search of a dragon. He tried to imagine all the excitement a dragon could bring to the kingdom. But all he could think about were burnt houses, roasted fields, and toasted villagers being eaten for lunch. He said he would do his best, but secretly, Sir Gordon hoped he *wouldn't* find a dragon.

For many days, Sir Gordon searched the countryside. Sometimes he would stop and ask people where he could find a dragon.

Sometimes they would look at him strangely.

Sometimes they would laugh at him.

Sometimes they would try to talk him out of it. They would tell him horrible stories about what dragons could do. Nobody knew where a dragon was or where one could be found. Nobody wanted to know.

Until . . .

"A dragon?" asked a farmer when Sir Gordon stopped to give Sturdy Roger a rest. "I don't know if it's a dragon, but I hear there's something big and dark and scary sneaking around in the woods beyond the next town."

Sir Gordon thanked the farmer and rode off.

He was so excited that he rushed past the town and was deep into the woods before he remembered to be a little scared. This was a *dragon* he was looking for, after all.

Then something big and dark and scary crawled out from behind some trees. Sir Gordon remembered to be very scared.

"Excuse me," said Sir Gordon in a voice sounding as brave as he could make it, "are you a dragon?"

"Heavens, no! I'm an ogre," said the creature. "Good grief, why do you want to find a dragon? They're horrible!"

Sir Gordon told the creature about the king's ideas for keeping a dragon.

"Yikes!" said the ogre. "Sounds like your king has been eating too many cookies. Maybe he would like an ogre in his kingdom instead. I could live under bridges, make horrible noises, and eat goats."

Sir Gordon scrunched up his face in disgust. "Why would the king want that?"

"Well, why would he want some big lizard eating everybody and burning his kingdom down?" asked the ogre.

The knight didn't have an answer for that question.

"Anyway," said the ogre, "I hear some dragons like high places. There's a mountain just beyond these woods. You should look there."

Sir Gordon thanked the ogre and told him he'd mention his "living under bridges, making noise, and eating goats" idea to the king

He then rode off to the mountain.

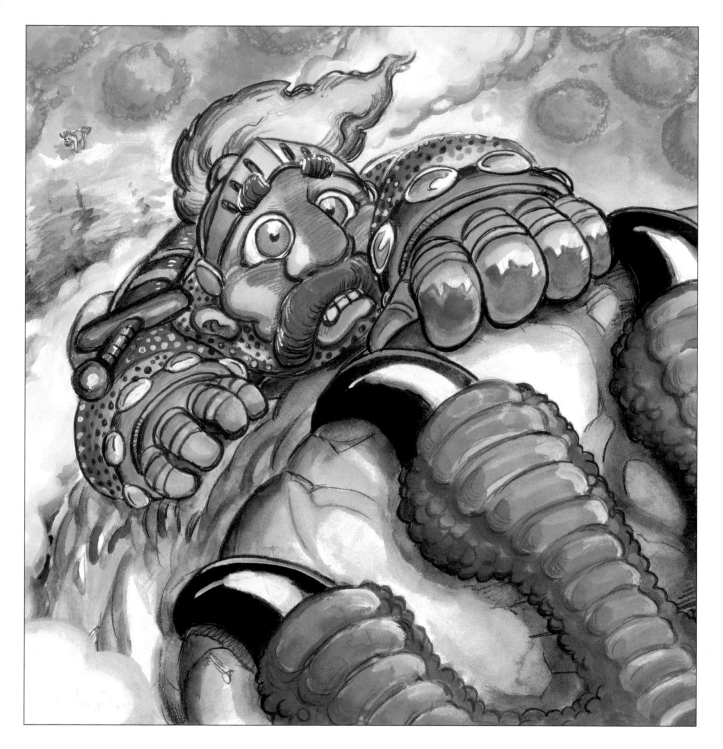

The mountain was very steep. Sir Gordon had to leave his horse Roger at the bottom while he climbed up to the rocky peak. It took a long time. The wind was very cold. The knight was tired and almost frozen by the time he reached the top.

He was just pulling himself up to the rocks at the very tip of the mountain when he saw something huge with large wings looking down at him.

"Excuse me," said Sir Gordon, trying hard not to sound cold and tired, "are you a dragon?"

"Nope, I'm a griffin," said the creature. "Dragons are big, ugly, lizard-things with more horns and more sharp claws than they know what to do with. I'm a more good-looking mix of a lion and an eagle. You can see that, can't you?"

Sir Gordon nodded. He was just too cold and tired to speak.

"Look, buddy, you can't stay here," said the griffin. "My eggs are hatching and my wife doesn't like intruders. Why don't I fly you back to your little horse down there and you can be on you way?"

Sir Gordon nodded again. He hadn't looked forward to climbing back down the mountain.

"Hmm, dragons," said the griffin as he carried the knight down from the sky. "I haven't seen any. But there's a valley to the east that looks black and burnt as if a dragon's breath had roasted it. You should try there." Sir Gordon thanked the griffin and wished him good luck with his egg hatching. He then pointed Sturdy Roger to the east and soon fell asleep while riding toward the valley.

There weren't any dragons in the black and burnt valley, but there were strange fairies called banshees. Sir Gordon tried to ask them about dragons but all they did was moan and wail at him.

Finally, one pretty little banshee stopped and said, "I don't think your king would be happy with a real dragon, they're too dangerous. Maybe he would like me to make him a *stuffed* one instead."

"I didn't know banshees could do anything besides moan and wail," said Sir Gordon.

" There's more to life than moaning and wailing," said the banshee as she showed the knight some stuffed toys she had made. "I think I am a pretty good toymaker."

Although Sir Gordon liked her toys, he knew that the king wanted a real dragon. "But I'll keep you in mind," he promised.

"Dragons like caves," said the banshee. "You should search the caves in those hills to the north." Sir Gordon kissed her cheek and headed north.

Trolls who lived in the caves had never even *heard* of dragons (they didn't get out much). They thanked Sir Gordon for telling them about such dangerous creatures and said they once met a goblin who had run away from something big and green that was crawling around in the lowlands swamp. Maybe *that* was a dragon.

"I'll ask that goblin," said the knight. "Where did he go?" "He didn't go anywhere," said the trolls. "We ate him." Sir Gordon quickly said good-bye and rode toward the swamp.

"Those stupid trolls thought I was a dragon?" laughed the vodyanoi in the swamp. "What a bunch of nincompoops! Dragons don't live in water. Well . . . unless they're *sea dragons. That's* where you should look, sir knight—in the sea!"

The mermaids he found in the sea thought the whole idea very funny. "Why would anyone want to capture a dragon?" they laughed as they splashed water on Sir Gordon, who didn't like being laughed at by little fish women. Sturdy Roger was getting seasick. So the knight rowed back to land, without even a clue as to where he should look next.

But he kept hunting since he was a loyal and hard-working knight
who always tried to do his best. He left no stone unturned.

He hunted in cold places.

He hunted in hot places.

He hunted in very, very strange places. But wherever he went, the story was the same. No dragons. No dragons at all.

Finally, Sir Gordon couldn't hunt anymore. He was tired, and lonely, and far, far away from home. "I hope my nephew will understand," he sighed.

"I have done my best, but I just can't find a dragon."

"Please take ours!" the king of another land said. "You want a dragon? There's one in my kingdom just up the road. The huge lizard is burning and eating everything in sight. We're leaving to build another kingdom far away and we're fed up with dragons! If you want ours, you're welcome to him."

"At last! At last!" cried Sir Gordon. He leaped on Sturdy Roger and charged toward the nearby kingdom.

They slowed to a trot as they entered the kingdom. Sir Gordon remembered how scared he was . . . he didn't really want to find a dragon.

And then he found a dragon.

"E-e-excuse me-me-me," said Sir Gordon, trying hard not to sound absolutely terrified, "are y-y-you a d-d-d-dragon?"

"Oh, yessss," hissed the dragon. "What do you want, my crunchy little knight?"

"M-m-my nephew, His M-M-Majesty King Edwin, invites you to attack our k-k-king-dom so he can have fun defending it from y-y-you."

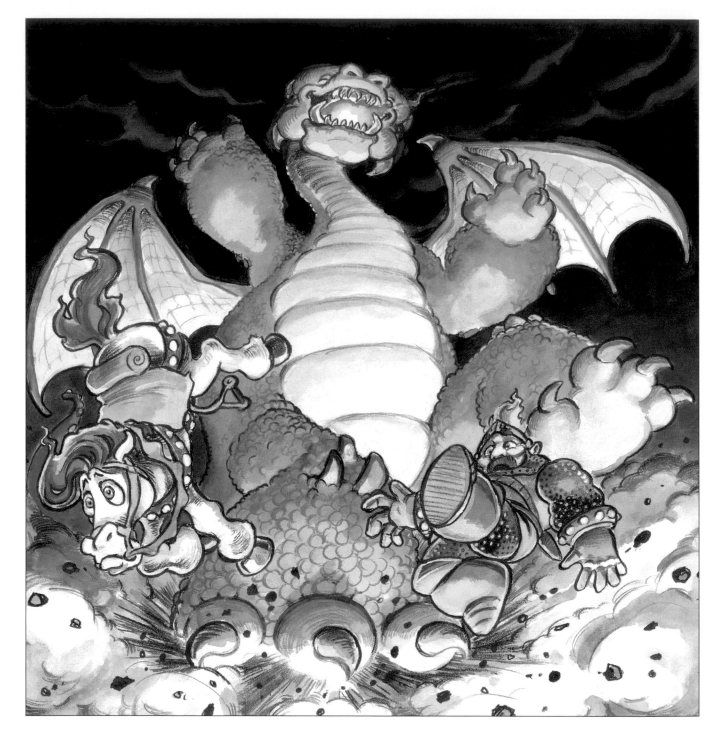

"You're . . . *inviting* me to attack his kingdom?" the dragon asked in amazement. "Why that's the best thing that's ever happened to me! No one has ever invited me anywhere!"

He danced around with excitement. "You won't be sorry!" I'll do my best work ever! I'll burn and destroy your land so well that no one will ever know there was ever a kingdom there!"

"When do you want me to start?"

And then Sir Gordon realized how stupid he was being.
He loved King Edwin so much he would get him anything he asked for,
but he loved his nephew too much to get him a dangerous ferocious dragon.

"Um . . . we'll send you a letter when we're ready to be attacked," said Sir Gordon, leaping on Sturdy Roger. "Stay here so we'll know where to address your letter."

"Okay," said the dragon, "but make it soon. There's nothing left to eat here. I'll starve if I stay too long, but I'm so excited by your invitation that I'll risk it. Write soon!"

"We'll let you know when we're ready!" called Sir Gordon as he raced Sturdy Roger away from the city as fast as he could go. He knew that it would be many years before the kingdom would be ready for a dragon attack. The dragon would have starved to death by then. Sir Gordon felt he was being rather sneaky, but he was saving his kingdom . . . and his nephew, the king.

On his was back home, Sir Gordon picked up the banshee who was a toymaker.

And Kind Edwin was happy with the dragon he finally got.

THE END

Ogre
(Giant)

Troll

Goblin

Mermaid
(Merrow)

Griffin

Peryton

anoi

Satyr

M

Ogre
(Cyclops)

Manticore

aur

Unicorn

Y

Harpy

Elf
(Fee)

Union Public Library
1980 Morris Avenue
Union, N.J. 07083

P9-DGJ-152

WILLIAMS-SONOMA

NEW FLAVORS FOR
appetizers

RECIPES
Amy Sherman

PHOTOGRAPHS
Tucker + Hossler

Union Public Library
1980 Morris Avenue
Union, N.J. 07083

Oxmoor
House.

spring

summer

fall

winter

introducing new flavors

Whether it's an hors d'oeuvre, salad, soup, or first course, today's appetizers are fresher and more interesting than ever before. Restaurant chefs, television food personalities, and food writers are pioneering this effort in two main ways: first, by insisting upon farm-fresh, local, and seasonally driven ingredients; and next, by incorporating bold global flavorings into their signature dishes to add unexpected flair. This book reveals how, just by employing these two simple tactics, you too can breathe new life into everyday dishes—and with surprisingly little effort.

Your local farmers' market or natural-foods' store can supply plenty of seasonal inspiration. Choosing fruits and vegetables according to their peak growing cycle guarantees high-impact flavor before you even start to cook. Bringing international accents into your kitchen requires just a trip to your local grocery store, ethnic market, or specialty-food store. There, you'll find that items once considered unusual, like smoked paprika, red or green curry paste, and wasabi, are now nearly as common finds as garlic, mustard, and nuts.

The forty-four appetizers that follow are organized according to the best season during which to make them, whether that is because the featured ingredients are at their peak of freshness and flavor, or because the season itself evokes a certain cooking style, for example, grilling in warm weather, or roasting and braising during the cool months. Of course, feel free to make the recipes on any day you choose if you can find fresh ingredients. We hope that the following classic recipes, refreshed with seasonal produce and high-impact ethnic seasonings, will re-inspire you to cook for yourself, your family, and your friends.

freshness as an ingredient

When food is fresh, it is already delicious, so it makes your job as a cook much easier. For the best-tasting appetizers, try to use ingredients that are in season, sourced from a nearby location, and, ideally, not treated with chemicals.

seasonal Cooking in rhythm with the seasons is not a new idea. Before mass transportation, people ate only what was proliferating in gardens, nearby farms, or in orchards. Today, produce is transported from all points of the globe in order to meet the demands of consumers. The problem is, while these items may look beautiful, their flavor does not compare with fruits or vegetables in their peak season—a bite of a mealy, tasteless supermarket tomato in February illustrates that point clearly.

local One way to ensure that the produce you purchase is at its freshest is to procure it from a local farmers' market or nearby farm stand, or a grocery store that has relationships with local farmers. Doing so practically guarantees that the melons in the bushel and the leeks tied in fat bunches were picked within hours of appearing at the market. Purchasing locally sourced fruits also means that the produce has less far to travel from farm or orchard to the store, which means the food can be picked closer to its natural peak. As such, it boasts a better and fuller flavor.

organic Choosing organic over conventional fruits, vegetables, dairy products, poultry, and meats is another sensible way to ensure good flavor. Organic foods aren't exposed to the chemicals and other substances available to conventional producers so they retain their true flavors. Organic produce generally does not have a long shelf life, so it must be rushed to market for immediate sale.

being bold

Start with fresh ingredients, and your appetizers need little to adorn them. Easy
ways to help your dishes shine include using bold seasonings, employing flavorful
cooking methods, and combining ingredients in surprising ways.

high-impact seasonings In contrast to using locally sourced produce, many
of the flavorings used in these recipes have been imported from other regions.
These global spices, seasoning pastes, cured meats and cheeses, and condiments
help bring an element of surprise to appetizers. For example, saffron lends an
exotic elegance to a dipping sauce for roasted baby artichokes. Spanish chorizo and
manchego stuffed into dates lend smoky and tart counterpoints to the sweet fruit.
Spicy Mexican chipotle chiles cleverly offset the sweetness of fresh corn fritters.

flavorful cooking methods The way in which appetizers are cooked can
also have a big impact on how they taste. Cooking foods on the stove top over very
high heat caramelizes their natural sugars, bringing a sweet flavor to the forefront.
Grilling foods, such as fresh figs, over a charcoal grill lends a measure of smokiness
to the dish. Braising foods, like winter greens and garlic, mellows any harsh flavors
and contributes a rich texture.

unexpected pairings Recipes become classics when they are reliable and
crowd-pleasing. This book reinterprets some of these same dishes with a surprising
ingredient—deviled eggs are accented with peppery watercress; baby lamb chops
feature a chunky mint-pistachio pesto instead of the standard mint jelly; apple
turnovers take a savory turn with the addition of cheddar cheese and fresh thyme.

flavors in layers

Utilizing fresh ingredients and seasoning them with a bold palette is only part of the story when creating high-impact appetizers. Layering the flavors, textures, and temperatures in complementary or contrasting ways helps bring all the parts into a unified whole. Creating these tiers of complexity within an appetizer can help modernize and redefine your dishes.

complement and contrast Many of the recipes were developed by layering ingredients with similar flavor components or ingredients with very different flavor profiles, in order to add depth and complexity to the dish. For example, tangy buttermilk counters the sweetness of garden-fresh peas in a quick cold soup; briny capers offset a rich mayonnaise sauce in a creative spin on lobster rolls; toasted hazelnuts reinforce the nutty impression of a citrus salad dressed with hazelnut oil.

texture and temperature Texture also plays a role in creating intriguing appetizers. Crisp fennel and crunchy radishes contrast with meaty fresh fish in a new spin on tuna tartare. A warm bacon vinaigrette drizzled over cool lettuces creates a wonderful take on an autumnal mushroom salad. A crunchy cornmeal tartlet crust lends a textural counterpoint to a creamy mushroom filling.

Remember that appetizers need not be complicated to be interesting. Choosing foods carefully and using them sensibly allows you to use a minimum of ingredients when cooking. Doing so with an intrepid spirit and in concert with the seasons will naturally bring the best results to your dishes. Let the recipes that follow be your inspiration as you embark on a flavor journey of your own.

spring

fava bean and ricotta crostini with fresh mint

fava beans in their pods,
1½ pounds

baguette, 1

whole-milk ricotta cheese,
½ cup

pecorino romano cheese,
½ cup finely grated

fresh mint, 1½ tablespoons chopped

lemon zest, ½ teaspoon finely grated

extra-virgin olive oil,
2 tablespoons, plus oil for drizzling

sea salt and freshly ground pepper

MAKES 16 CROSTINI;
3–4 SERVINGS

Preheat the oven to 400°F.

Shell the fava beans. Bring a saucepan three-fourths full of water to a boil over high heat. Add the beans and boil until tender, about 5 minutes. Drain into a colander and then rinse under cold running water until cool. Remove the outer skin from each bean by pinching open the end opposite where the fava bean attaches to the pod. You should have about 1 cup shelled and skinned beans. Finely chop the beans and add them to a bowl.

Cut the baguette into 16 slices, each ½ inch thick, reserve any remaining baguette for another use. Arrange the baguette slices on a rimmed baking sheet and toast in the oven until crisp, turning once, about 5 minutes total. Remove from the oven and set aside.

Add the ricotta, pecorino, 1 tablespoon of the mint, lemon zest, and 2 tablespoons olive oil to the bowl with the fava beans. Using a fork, mash the ingredients together until well blended. Season to taste with salt and pepper.

Heap a spoonful of the bean mixture onto each baguette toast. Drizzle lightly with olive oil and sprinkle with the remaining mint. Arrange the toasts on a platter and serve right away.

A creamy base of ricotta cheese makes a perfect foil for fava beans' slightly "green" flavor in this creative crostini topping. Fresh mint is a classic partner to favas in a variety of Mediterranean cuisines. Its refreshing taste is set off here by sharp pecorino and fragrant lemon zest.

olives and feta marinated with lemon and ouzo

Here, a trio of classic Greek ingredients— mildly sweet anise-flavored ouzo, pleasantly briny feta cheese, and rich, meaty Kalamata olives—delivers bold, distinctive tastes that heighten the appetite for the dishes that follow.

Place the olives in a bowl. Cut the cheese into roughly ½-inch cubes and add them to the olives. Finely dice the lemon, including the peel, and remove any seeds with the tip of the knife. Add the lemon, garlic to taste, olive oil, and ouzo to the olives and cheese, and mix gently with a wooden spoon. Cover lightly and let the mixture stand at room temperature for at least 1 hour to blend the flavors. (Alternatively, you can store the dish in a covered container in the refrigerator for up to 1 week; bring to room temperature before serving.)

Add the parsley leaves, mix gently, and serve right away, providing napkins or toothpicks for serving.

kalamata olives, ½ pound, pitted

feta cheese, preferably greek, ¼ pound

lemon, ½

garlic, 1–2 cloves, minced

fruity extra-virgin olive oil, ¼ cup

ouzo, ¼ cup

fresh flat-leaf parsley leaves, from ¼ bunch

MAKES 10–12 SERVINGS

Herbal asparagus and oniony leeks lend their iconic spring flavors to a baked quiche-like mixture of mild ricotta, tart chèvre, and a farm-fresh egg. The absence of a crust lets the other ingredients shine in these creative savory bites.

baked asparagus, leek, and goat cheese bites

unsalted butter,
2½ teaspoons, plus butter for greasing

asparagus, 6 spears, tough ends trimmed

leek, 1, halved lengthwise, white and light green parts finely chopped

fresh goat cheese, 2 ounces

whole-milk ricotta cheese, ½ cup

large egg, 1

MAKES 12 BITES,
6–12 SERVINGS

Preheat the oven to 300°F. Generously coat the cups of a 12-cup miniature muffin pan with butter.

Thinly slice the asparagus spears crosswise, keeping the tips whole. Set the asparagus tips aside.

In a sauté pan over medium-low heat, melt 2 teaspoons of the butter. Add the sliced asparagus and the leek and cook gently, stirring often, until just softened slightly, 1–2 minutes. Transfer to a small bowl and let cool.

Crumble the goat cheese into a bowl. Add the ricotta cheese and egg and mash together with a fork until well combined, and then mix in the cooled vegetables. Divide the filling evenly among the prepared muffin cups. Bake the "bites" until puffed and lightly golden on top, 20–25 minutes.

Meanwhile, cut each asparagus tip in half lengthwise. In a small nonstick frying pan over low heat, melt the remaining ½ teaspoon butter. Add the asparagus tips and sauté just until tender, about 1 minute. Transfer to a small bowl and set aside.

When the bites are done, transfer the pan to a wire rack. Run a table knife around the inside of each cup to loosen the edges, and then let cool slightly. Invert a large plate or tray over the muffin pan, invert the pan and plate together, and lift off the pan.

Arrange the bites on a platter or individual plates and top each with an asparagus-tip half. Serve warm or at room temperature.

Choose a soft, crumbly, fresh goat cheese with a hint of citrus to highlight the onion-like leeks and earthy asparagus in this dish. The freshest whole-milk ricotta available will provide these eggy mouthfuls the creamiest, lightest texture.

deviled eggs with watercress

Bright herbal nuances characterize this modern take on an old-fashioned favorite. Organic eggs that reveal buttery orange yolks when cooked yield a particularly handsome filling, with the cool, refreshing tang of watercress and tart lemon zest cutting their natural richness.

Place the eggs in a single layer in a saucepan. Add cold water to cover the eggs by at least 1 inch, place over medium heat, and bring to a boil. When the water is at a full boil, immediately remove the pan from the heat, cover, and let stand for 15 minutes.

Uncover the pan and place under cold running water until the eggs are cool. Drain the eggs, peel, and cut in half lengthwise. Using the tip of a spoon, carefully dislodge the yolks, allowing them to fall into a bowl. Set the whites aside, hollow side up. Mash the yolks with a fork until very smooth.

Discard the tough stems from the watercress and mince enough of the leaves to measure ¼ cup. Add the minced watercress, green onion, lemon zest, and mayonnaise to the yolks and mix well with a fork. The mixture should have a smooth, creamy consistency. Season to taste with salt.

Arrange the egg whites on a serving platter. Using a small spoon, divide the egg yolk mixture among the egg whites, mounding the mixture slightly in the centers. Serve right away.

large eggs, 6

watercress, 1 large bunch

green onion, 1, white and pale green parts minced

lemon zest, 1 teaspoon finely grated

homemade mayonnaise (page 144), 3 tablespoons

sea salt

MAKES 12 DEVILED EGGS; 4–6 SERVINGS

Though expensive, just a few threads of saffron add vibrant flavor and an appealing yellow color to dishes. Even a simple mayonnaise sauce for roasted baby artichokes gains a unique exotic flair when infused with the spice.

roasted baby artichokes with meyer lemon—saffron aioli

meyer lemon, 1 large

baby artichokes, 2 pounds (about 25)

extra-virgin olive oil, ¼ cup

sea salt and freshly ground pepper

saffron threads, pinch

homemade mayonnaise (page 144), ¼ cup

garlic, 1 clove, minced

MAKES 10–12 SERVINGS

Preheat the oven to 425°F. Line a rimmed baking sheet with aluminum foil. Bring a large pot three-fourths full of water to boil over high heat.

Halve the lemon and squeeze 1 tablespoon juice; set the juice aside. Fill a large bowl three-fourths full with water and squeeze the remaining lemon juice into the water. Working with 1 artichoke at a time, snap off the dark green outer leaves until you reach the pale green center. Using a sharp knife, trim the stem, and then cut off about ½ inch from the top to remove the spiny tips. Cut the artichoke in half lengthwise and drop the artichoke pieces into the lemon water to prevent discoloration. Repeat with the remaining artichokes.

Drain the artichokes, add them to the boiling water, and cook until just tender when pierced with a knife, about 5 minutes. Drain well in a colander and let cool slightly. In a bowl, combine the warm artichokes, olive oil, and a light sprinkle of salt and pepper and toss to coat evenly. Pour onto the prepared baking sheet and spread into a single layer. Roast until the artichokes turn brown on the bottom and edges, 10–15 minutes.

Meanwhile, in a small bowl, soak the saffron in 1 tablespoon hot water. In another bowl, combine the mayonnaise, garlic, reserved lemon juice, and the saffron with its soaking water. Mix well and season to taste with salt.

Remove the artichokes from the oven and let cool slightly. Arrange the artichokes on a warmed serving platter with the mayonnaise mixture, or aioli, alongside for dipping. Serve right away.

Lightly herbal artichokes are roasted to bring out both a natural nuttiness and sweetness in the vegetable. They're then paired with perfumed saffron and the sweet-sour juice of last-of-the-season Meyer lemons in a rich dipping sauce. If Meyer lemons are no longer available, use regular lemons and add a drop of honey to the sauce.

cold pea soup with crème fraîche and chives

In this refreshing chilled soup, faintly oniony fresh chives and the light tang of both buttermilk and crème fraîche enhance fresh spring peas without overwhelming their delicate nature.

Shell the peas, pressing your thumb against the seam of each pod to force it open. You should have 2 cups shelled peas. Bring a saucepan three-fourths full of water to a boil over high heat. Add the peas and boil until bright green and tender, 2–3 minutes. Drain through a large sieve, rinse under cold running water until cool, then drain well.

Tear the lettuce into small pieces. In a blender, combine the peas, lettuce pieces, buttermilk, and 1½ teaspoons salt and process until completely smooth. Pour the soup into a bowl, cover, and refrigerate until well chilled and the flavors are blended, about 2 hours.

Using kitchen shears, snip the chives into very small pieces. Stir the crème fraîche with a fork so it is fluid. Divide the soup evenly among chilled small soup bowls. Spoon the crème fraîche onto each serving, dividing evenly. Sprinkle each serving with some of the chopped chives. Serve right away.

english peas in their pods, 2 pounds

butter lettuce, 5 large leaves

buttermilk, 2 cups

sea salt

fresh chives, ½ bunch

crème fraîche (page 144 or purchased) or sour cream, ½ cup

MAKES 6–8 SERVINGS

chilled poached **shrimp** with zesty balsamic dipping sauce

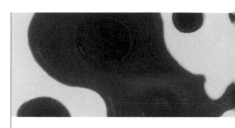

lemons, 1½

organic ketchup, ⅔ cup

cream-style horseradish,
1–2 teaspoons

soy sauce, 1 teaspoon

balsamic vinegar,
½ teaspoon

worcestershire sauce,
½ teaspoon

dry mustard, ¼ teaspoon

hot red-pepper sauce

peppercorns, ½ teaspoon

large shrimp in the shell,
16–20 (1 pound total
weight)

MAKES 4–6 SERVINGS

Squeeze 1 teaspoon juice from the lemon half. In a small bowl, whisk together the lemon juice, ketchup, horseradish, soy sauce, vinegar, Worcestershire sauce, mustard, and pepper sauce to taste until thoroughly mixed. Cover and refrigerate for at least 30 minutes or up to overnight to blend the flavors.

Cut the remaining lemon into quarters. Fill a large stockpot one-half full with water and add the lemon quarters and peppercorns. Bring to a boil over high heat, add the shrimp, cover, and bring back to a boil. Reduce the heat to medium and simmer for 1 minute; the shrimp should be just opaque. Drain into a colander and rinse under cold running water until cool.

To peel the shrimp, carefully pull off and discard the head if still attached. Then, pull apart the legs and gently pull off the shell, working from the top to the tail and leaving the tail segments intact. Using a small sharp knife, cut a shallow channel in the back of the shrimp and pull away the dark vein-like tract with the tip of the knife. Place the shrimp in a bowl, cover, and refrigerate for at least 10 minutes or for up to 6 hours.

Arrange the chilled shrimp on a platter with the sauce alongside for dipping. Serve right away.

A hint of sweet balsamic vinegar in this tomato-based sauce lends traditional shrimp cocktail an upscale edge. Mild fresh shrimp, gently poached, is the perfect vehicle for the sour, spicy, salty, and sweet elements in the assertive sauce.

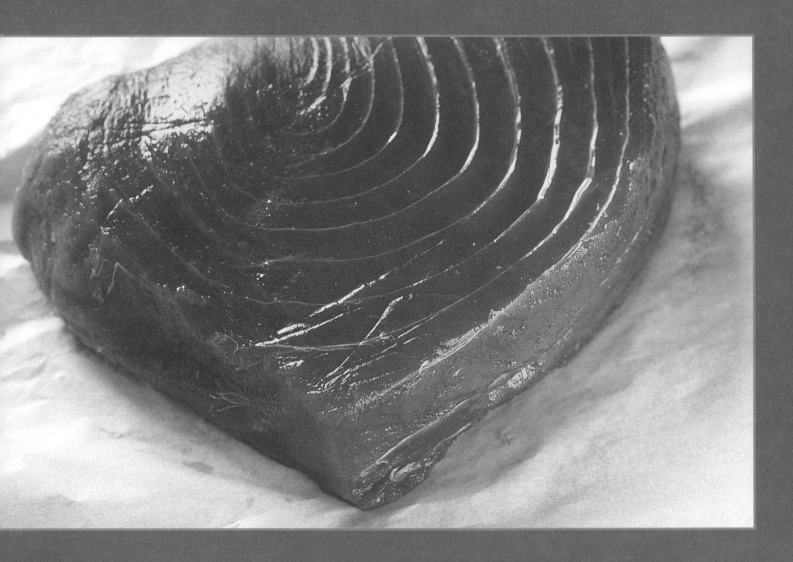

Meatlike fresh tuna is a neutral canvas onto which many contrasting elements can be applied. Here, it becomes a light, refreshing take on steak tartare with crunchy fresh fennel, crisp, sharp radishes, and a simple citrus dressing.

tuna crudo with fennel and radishes

sushi-grade ahi tuna,
1 pound, well chilled

fennel, 1 large or 2 small
bulbs

radishes, 1 bunch (about 8)

fresh lemon juice, ¼ cup

**peppery extra-virgin
olive oil,** ½ cup

**sea salt and freshly ground
pepper**

MAKES 8 SERVINGS

Leave the tuna in the refrigerator until you are ready to cut it. If it is well chilled, it will be easier to work with.

If the fennel stalks are still attached, trim them and reserve for another use or discard. Reserve a few of the feathery fronds for garnish, if desired. Remove and discard the outer layer of the fennel bulb if it is tough, or cut away any discolored areas. Halve the bulb lengthwise and trim the base of the core. Trim off the leafy tops and the root ends from the radishes. Using a mandoline or large sharp knife, cut the fennel bulb halves and then the radishes into paper-thin slices.

Using a long, sharp knife, and cutting with the grain, cut the tuna into ½-inch dice, removing any sinew.

Divide the fennel and radishes evenly among chilled small bowls or plates. If desired, roughly chop some of the fennel fronds and add a few to each bowl. Arrange the tuna on top of the vegetables, again dividing evenly. In a small bowl, whisk together the lemon juice and oil until blended. Drizzle the lemon-oil mixture evenly over the tuna and vegetables and season lightly with salt and pepper. Serve right away.

Here, a bouquet of markedly different tastes——sweet, anise-scented fennel, sharp radishes, and tart citrus——are tied together with peppery olive oil. They accompany small cubes of ahi tuna, also known as yellowfin tuna, whose rich, meaty flavor is enhanced by the vibrant, contrasting accompaniments.

seared sea scallops with coconut–red curry sauce

Spicy curry paste, salty fish sauce, caramel-like brown sugar and rich coconut milk combine in a sauce to coat rich sea scallops. Served on a bed of faintly bitter baby spinach, it becomes an exotic first course for entertaining.

Discard any tough stems from the spinach and rinse well. Set aside.

In a large frying pan over medium heat, melt 1 tablespoon of the butter. Add the scallops, sprinkle lightly with salt and pepper, and brown well on the first sides, about 2 minutes. Turn the scallops over, sprinkle with salt and pepper, and cook until brown on the second sides but still translucent in the center, 1–2 minutes longer. Transfer to a plate.

Wipe out the pan, return it to medium heat, and melt the remaining 1 tablespoon butter. Add the coconut milk and ½ teaspoon red curry paste and bring to a simmer, stirring to distribute the curry paste. Simmer until the coconut milk has reduced by half, a few minutes. Add the fish sauce and brown sugar and stir well. Remove from the heat and keep warm.

Place the spinach, with the rinsing water still clinging to the leaves, in a large saucepan over medium-high heat. Cover and cook the spinach, turning the leaves two or three times, until wilted, 3–5 minutes. Remove from the heat and set aside, covered.

Return the scallops and any juices that have accumulated to the frying pan with the sauce and sauté until the scallops are just cooked through, about 1 minute. Season to taste with up to ½ teaspoon more curry paste or with more sugar and fish sauce.

Drain the spinach well in a sieve, and then divide it among warmed individual plates. Using a slotted spoon, arrange 2 scallops on top of each serving. Drizzle the sauce over the tops and serve right away.

baby spinach, about 10 ounces

unsalted butter, 2 tablespoons

large sea scallops, 12 (about 1 pound total weight)

sea salt and freshly ground pepper

unsweetened coconut milk, 1 cup

red curry paste, ½–1 teaspoon

thai fish sauce, 1 teaspoon, or to taste

brown sugar, ½ teaspoon, or to taste

MAKES 6 SERVINGS

slow-roasted pork tostaditas with pickled red onions

red onion, 1, cut into ⅛-inch rings

boiling water, 2 cups

fresh orange juice, 1⅔ cups, or as needed

cider vinegar, ⅓ cup

kosher salt, ¼ teaspoon

boneless pork shoulder, about 2¼ pounds

garlic, 3 cloves, minced

ground cumin, 1 teaspoon

sea salt, ¾ teaspoon

red pepper flakes, ½ teaspoon

low-sodium chicken broth, 1 cup

hass avocado, 1 large

fresh cilantro, 1 bunch

organic tortilla chips, 1 bag (10 ounces)

MAKES 36–40 TOSTADITAS, ABOUT 12 SERVINGS

Place the onion rings in a small heatproof bowl and pour the boiling water over the top. Let stand until softened, about 10 minutes. Drain the onion slices well and return them to the bowl. Add ⅔ cup of the orange juice, the vinegar, and the kosher salt and stir well. Add more orange juice if the onion slices are not submerged. Cover and let stand at room temperature for at least 2 hours or up to 8 hours.

Preheat the oven to 300°F. Cut the pork into 1-inch cubes and add them to a bowl. Add the garlic, cumin, sea salt, and red pepper flakes and toss to coat the meat evenly. Spread the pork in a 9-by-13-inch nonreactive roasting pan and pour in the remaining 1 cup orange juice and the broth. Cover the pan tightly with aluminum foil and roast the pork for 2 hours.

Uncover the pan and continue to roast, stirring occasionally, until the pork is very tender when a meat fork is inserted into the center, about 1 hour longer. Remove from the oven and let cool slightly.

Using your hands or 2 forks, pull the pork apart to make small shreds. Cover with aluminum foil to keep warm.

Halve, pit, and peel the avocado, and then cut into quarters. Cut each quarter lengthwise into about 10 slices. Pluck about 40 nice-sized cilantro leaves from their stems.

To assemble the tostaditas, arrange 36–40 chips on a serving platter. Mound a spoonful of roasted pork on top of each chip. Lay a thin slice of avocado on the meat, and then top with a pickled onion ring. Garnish each tostadita with a cilantro leaf and serve right away.

Pork rubbed with a combination of sweet and savory seasonings emerges rich and aromatic from a slow oven. Shredded, it is then layered with buttery avocado, pickled red onion, herbal cilantro, and crunchy tortilla chips for a creative, Mexican-inspired hors d'oeuvre.

A clever twist on classic pesto pairs the subtle nuttiness of pistachio nuts with the refreshing flavor of just-picked mint. The result is a modern alternative to mint jelly for spring lamb chops, simply seasoned and briefly cooked.

pan-seared spring lamb chops with mint-pistachio pesto

fresh mint leaves, 1 cup packed

fresh flat-leaf parsley leaves, ¼ cup packed

shelled, salted roasted pistachio nuts, ¼ cup

garlic, 1 clove, roughly chopped

fruity extra-virgin olive oil, ½ cup, plus oil for browning

sea salt

small lamb rib chops, frenched, 12

MAKES 6 SERVINGS

In a food processor or blender, combine the mint, parsley, pistachio nuts, garlic, and ½ cup olive oil and process until blended but still retains some texture. Transfer the mixture to a bowl and season to taste with salt. You should have about ¾ cup pesto.

Preheat the oven to 200°F. In a large, heavy frying pan over medium heat, warm about 1 tablespoon olive oil. Add as many lamb chops to the pan as will fit without crowding and cook, turning once, until well browned on both sides and done to your liking, about 5 minutes on each side for medium-rare. Transfer to a plate and place in the oven to keep warm. Repeat to cook the remaining lamb chops.

To serve, arrange the lamb chops on a warmed platter or divide them among warmed serving plates (2 chops per serving). Top each chop with a dollop of pesto. Pass the remaining pesto with the platter or at the table, or reserve for another use. Serve right away.

The pistachios in this chunky herb paste give it an unexpected boost of earthy flavor. Fragrant fresh mint provides an intriguing herbal zing, accented by pungent garlic. When paired, this new take on pesto enhances the delicate but distinctive taste of seared lamb chops.

summer

cucumber and avocado summer rolls with mustard-soy sauce

lime juice, from ½ lime

rice bran or canola oil,
2 tablespoons

rice vinegar, 1 tablespoon

dijon mustard, ½ teaspoon

soy sauce, ½ teaspoon

brown sugar, 1 teaspoon

hass avocados, 2

rice paper rounds, 20,
6 or 8 inches in diameter

green leaf lettuce,
10 leaves

fresh basil leaves, from
1 bunch

fresh mint leaves, from
1 bunch

carrots, 2, coarsely
shredded

english cucumber, ½, cut
into thin strips

MAKES 20 ROLLS;
8–10 SERVINGS

In a small bowl, stir together the lime juice, oil, vinegar, mustard, soy sauce, and brown sugar until the sugar dissolves; set aside. Halve, pit, and peel the avocados, and then cut them into ½-inch dice.

Place a wide, shallow bowl of warm water on the work surface. Lay a kitchen towel next to the bowl. Dip one rice paper round into the water for a few seconds to soften, and then lay it flat on the towel. Dip a second round in the water and lay it directly on top of the first one. Using another towel, pat the top of the rice paper dry.

Center a lettuce leaf on top of the stacked rice papers. Starting about one-third in from the edge closest to you, arrange a few of the basil and mint leaves in a line across the lettuce. Top with a small row each of the carrots, cucumber, and avocado; be careful not to overstuff the roll. Lift the bottom edge of the rice paper up and over the filling and then roll once to form a tight cylinder. Fold in the sides of the rice paper and continue to roll the paper and filling into a tight cylinder. Set aside, seam side down. Repeat with the remaining rice paper and filling ingredients to make 10 rolls.

Cut each roll in half crosswise and arrange, cut side up, on a platter. Place the sauce alongside for dipping and serve right away.

Rich, nutty avocado is a great carrier of flavors, like the fresh herbs and cooling cucumber that star in these fresh rice-paper rolls. The savory dipping sauce features tart, sweet, and salty ingredients that mimic an exotic salad dressing— fitting, as these rolls are like a salad that is eaten out of hand.

avocado, toasted corn, and chipotle salsa

Toasting sweet corn in a hot pan lends a nuttiness to offset its natural sweetness. Here it is combined with tart tomatoes, buttery avocados, and a trio of Mexican flavorings— musky cumin, spicy-smoky chipotle chiles, and bright cilantro—for a fresh, colorful partner for crisp tortilla chips.

Remove the husks and silk from the corn. Using a large, sharp knife, carefully cut the ear in half crosswise. One at a time, stand the halves, flat end down, on a cutting board and cut the kernels from the cob.

In a large frying pan over medium heat, warm the olive oil. Add the corn kernels and sauté until the kernels are golden brown, about 10 minutes. Transfer to a bowl and let cool.

Halve, pit, and peel the avocados, and then cut them into ½-inch dice. Add them to a bowl with the corn kernels, tomato, green onions, and cilantro and toss to mix. In a small bowl, whisk together ½ teaspoon of the chipotle, the cumin, and vinegar and pour over the corn mixture. Toss gently and season to taste with salt and additional chipotle, if desired.

Transfer the salsa to a serving bowl and arrange the tortilla chips alongside. Serve right away, or cover and refrigerate for up to several hours. Bring to room temperature before serving.

sweet corn, 1 large ear

olive oil, 1 tablespoon

hass avocados, 2 small or 1 large

tomato, 1, diced

green onions, 2, white and tender greens cut into ¼-inch pieces

fresh cilantro, ½ cup chopped

chipotle chile in adobo sauce, ½–1 teaspoon minced

ground cumin, 1 teaspoon

red wine vinegar, 1 teaspoon

sea salt

organic tortilla chips for serving

MAKES ABOUT 3 CUPS; 6–8 SERVINGS

A Spanish version of the classic prosciutto-and-melon antipasto combines paper-thin slices of serrano ham with cubes of seedless watermelon. Add squares of the native Manchego cheese for an easy hors d'oeuvre with high-impact flavor.

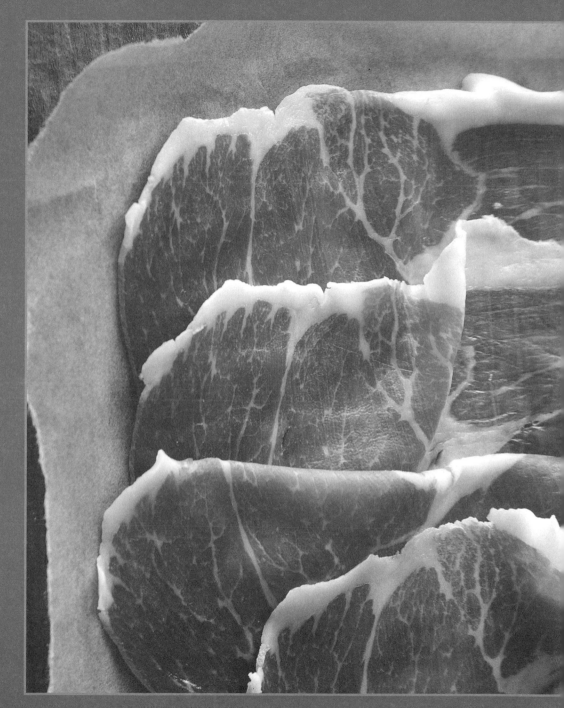

watermelon, manchego, and serrano ham skewers

Here, sweet watermelon is matched with sharp Manchego cheese and salty, meaty serrano ham. Assembled together into bite-sized morsels and finished with piquant black pepper, the ingredients mingle to create simple, yet bold, appetite sparkers.

Cut the melon flesh away from the rind. Discard the rind and cut the flesh into 1-inch cubes. Cut the ham into thin strips about ½ inch wide. Trim the rind off the cheese and discard. Cut the cheese into thin squares to fit the top of the watermelon cubes.

To assemble the skewers, place a piece of cheese on top of a watermelon cube, and then carefully top with 1 or 2 folded strips of ham. Secure each bite with a cocktail pick.

To serve, arrange the skewers on a platter, grind pepper generously over the top, and drizzle a drop or two of olive oil over each piece. Serve right away.

seedless watermelon, 1¼ pounds

serrano ham, ½ pound, thinly sliced

manchego cheese, 5 ounces

freshly ground pepper

extra-virgin olive oil

MAKES ABOUT 40 SKEWERS, 10–12 SERVINGS

smoky eggplant dip with cumin-crusted pita chips

extra-virgin olive oil

globe eggplants, 2 (about 2 pounds total weight)

garlic, 6 cloves, unpeeled

fresh lemon juice, 2 tablespoons

tahini, ¼ cup

sea salt

smoked sweet or hot paprika, ¼ teaspoon

cumin-crusted pita chips (page 144)

MAKES 8 SERVINGS

Place an oven rack 4–5 inches below the heating element and preheat the broiler. Line a broiler pan with aluminum foil and lightly grease the foil with oil. Cut the eggplants in half lengthwise and place, cut side down, on the prepared pan. Broil until the skins char and the eggplant flesh is tender, about 20 minutes. Transfer the eggplant to a colander and set it in the sink to drain and cool slightly.

Turn the oven temperature to 400°F. Trim off the stem ends of the garlic. Place the cloves on a small square of aluminum foil, drizzle with 1 teaspoon olive oil, and wrap the cloves securely in the foil. Bake until the garlic is soft when tested with a small knife, about 15 minutes. Unwrap the garlic and let stand until cool enough to handle. Leave the oven on.

Using a spoon, scrape the eggplant flesh out of the skins into a blender. Squeeze the garlic from its peels and add to the blender along with the lemon juice, tahini, and a scant ¼ teaspoon salt. Blend the ingredients until smooth, and then season to taste with salt. Transfer the dip to a serving bowl and let stand for a few minutes to blend the flavors.

To serve, garnish the dip with the smoked paprika and place on a platter. Arrange the pita chips alongside and serve right away.

Broiling the eggplant and charring the skin introduces smoky, earthy nuances, which come through in this vibrant dish. Roasted garlic mirrors the melting texture of the eggplant, its mellow sweetness helping to soften and balance the bright lemon and nutty sesame tahini in this exotic dip.

Mexican chipotles, actually smoked red jalapeños, and the vinegary adobo sauce they are packed in, lend a vibrant counter-point to sweet ingredients. Here, crisp fritters made from fresh corn create a pleasing contrast to a chipotle-spiked dipping sauce.

sweet corn fritters with smoky honey dipping sauce

homemade mayonnaise
(page 144), 1/2 cup

honey, 1/4 cup

chipotle chile in adobo
sauce, 1 1/2 teaspoons
minced

white corn, 3 ears

sweet rice flour, 1/2 cup

all-purpose flour, 1/2 cup

baking powder,
1/2 teaspoon

ground cumin, 1/2 teaspoon

sea salt, 1/2 teaspoon

large egg, 1

green onions, 2, white and
pale green parts minced

rice bran or canola oil for
frying

MAKES 18 FRITTERS;
4–6 SERVINGS

In a small bowl, stir together the mayonnaise, honey, and minced chipotle chile and mix well. Cover and set aside until serving.

Place a wire rack on a rimmed baking sheet, put the sheet in the oven, and preheat the oven to 250°F.

Remove the husks and silk from the ears of corn. Using a large, sharp knife, carefully cut each ear in half crosswise. One at a time, stand the halves, flat end down, on a cutting board and cut the kernels from the cob.

In a bowl, whisk together the rice flour, all-purpose flour, baking powder, cumin, and salt. Add the egg and 1/2 cup water and whisk until smooth. Add the corn kernels and green onions to the bowl and stir just until combined. The batter will be very thick.

Pour the oil into a large, heavy frying pan to a depth of 1/4 inch and warm over medium-high heat. Working in batches, spoon 1 tablespoon of the batter into the hot oil to form each fritter, spacing the fritters about 1/2 inch apart. Fry until golden brown on the first sides, about 2 minutes. Using a slotted spatula, carefully flip the fritters over and fry until golden brown on the second sides, about 2 minutes longer. Transfer the fritters to the baking sheet to drain and keep warm in the oven. Repeat with the remaining batter, adding more oil to the pan as needed.

Arrange the fritters on a warmed platter and place the dipping sauce alongside. Serve right away.

Farm-fresh white corn, at its sweetest in late summer, stars in this simple fritter, made extra-crisp by the addition of rice flour to the batter. Customize the sweet-smoky-spicy dipping sauce by using a distinctive honey, such as Tupelo, lavender, or sage.

grilled chicken skewers with peanut-ginger sauce

Rich, creamy coconut milk balances an intriguing combination of flavors in this bold, ginger-spiked peanut sauce. Some of the sauce is used as a marinade to pump up the mild taste of chicken breasts. The rest is cooked for a few minutes to gain intensity and then perfectly complement the grilled chicken skewers as a dipping sauce.

Soak twenty 6-inch bamboo skewers in water to cover for at least 30 minutes.

Prepare a charcoal or gas grill for direct-heat grilling over medium heat. Cut each chicken tender in half on the diagonal. Drain the skewers. Thread a chicken piece onto each skewer and place in a nonreactive baking dish.

In a small bowl, combine the garlic, ginger, lemon juice, peanut butter, brown sugar, coconut milk, ¼ cup water, soy sauce, sesame oil, and red pepper flakes and whisk until smooth. Pour ¼ cup of the sauce mixture over the chicken. Turn to coat the chicken in the mixture and marinate at room temperature for 10 minutes.

Transfer the remaining sauce mixture to a small saucepan and cook over low heat, stirring occasionally, until thickened, about 5 minutes. Remove from the heat and keep warm.

Remove the chicken skewers from the marinade and discard the marinade. Brush the grill rack with canola oil, then grill the chicken over direct heat just until cooked through, about 2 minutes on each side.

Arrange the skewers on a warmed platter. Pour the sauce over the skewers, or pour it into a small bowl and set alongside for dipping. Sprinkle the skewers with the peanuts, if desired, and serve right away.

chicken tenders, 1 pound

garlic, 1 clove, finely grated

fresh ginger, ½-inch piece, peeled and finely grated

fresh lemon juice, 1 tablespoon

natural peanut butter, ¼ cup

brown sugar, 1 tablespoon firmly packed

unsweetened coconut milk, ¼ cup

soy sauce, 2 teaspoons

asian sesame oil, 1 teaspoon

red pepper flakes, ¼ teaspoon

canola oil for grilling

roasted peanuts, 1 teaspoon chopped (optional)

MAKES 20 SKEWERS; 4–6 SERVINGS

lobster rolls with bacon, tomato, and caper mayonnaise

homemade mayonnaise (page 144), ½ cup

dijon mustard, ½ teaspoon

capers, 1½ teaspoons, drained and coarsely chopped

fresh flat-leaf parsley, 2 teaspoons finely chopped

anchovy paste, ¼ teaspoon

high-quality bacon, 6 slices

small soft rolls, 6, ideally oblong in shape

tomatoes, 2 small, diced

freshly cooked lobster meat, ½ pound, cut or torn into small chunks

MAKES 6 SANDWICHES; 3 OR 6 SERVINGS

In a small bowl, combine the mayonnaise, mustard, capers, parsley, and anchovy paste and stir to mix well. Set aside.

In a frying pan over medium heat, cook the bacon, turning as needed, just until crisp, 8–10 minutes. Meanwhile, split the rolls in half horizontally, leaving one side intact. Pull out most of the crumb from each half to create space for the filling. Transfer the cooked bacon to paper towels to drain.

When cool enough to handle, crumble the bacon into small pieces. Spread the cut sides of each roll with some of the mayonnaise mixture. Gently mix the lobster with the remaining mayonnaise mixture. Divide the lobster mixture evenly among the rolls. Top with the bacon and diced tomato, dividing evenly.

Close the rolls and press the sandwiches slightly to compress. Arrange on a platter and serve right away.

Capers lend their unique piquancy to the rich, mayonnaise-based spread in these petite sandwiches, adding a zesty counterpoint to luxurious lobster. Smoky, salty bacon and tart fresh tomatoes are the perfect accent for the crustacean's sweet, rich meat.

The beauty of this sauce is its pure, concentrated taste. Tomatoes and onions are first roasted to bring out their natural sweetness, puréed with bold seasonings, and then simmered together to bring all the flavors into a unified whole.

mini burgers with smoky tomato chutney

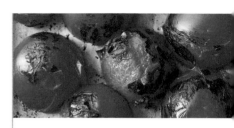

tomatoes, 1 pound, cored and halved crosswise

red onion, 1 small, unpeeled, cut into quarters

golden raisins, ¼ cup, coarsely chopped

sugar, ¼ cup

cider vinegar, ¼ cup

smoked paprika, 1 teaspoon

ground cumin, ½ teaspoon

sea salt

garlic, 1 clove, chopped

ground beef, 85 percent lean, 1 pound

fresh thyme, 1 tablespoon minced

worcestershire sauce, ¼ teaspoon

unsalted butter, 2 tablespoons, frozen

small dinner rolls, 8, about 3 inches in diameter

MAKES 8 MINI BURGERS;
3–4 SERVINGS

Place an oven rack 4–5 inches below the heating element and preheat the broiler. Arrange the tomato halves and onion quarters, skin side up, on a rimmed baking sheet. Broil until the skins begin to char, about 15 minutes.

In a small saucepan over very low heat, gently simmer the raisins, sugar, vinegar, paprika, cumin, and ¼ teaspoon salt, stirring occasionally, until the raisins begin to plump, about 5 minutes. Remove from the heat.

Remove and discard the peel from the onion quarters and put them in a blender. Add the garlic and charred tomatoes with their skins and process until a smooth purée forms. Pour the mixture into the saucepan with the raisin mixture, place over medium heat, and simmer, stirring occasionally, until thick, about 15 minutes. Season to taste with salt.

Preheat the oven to 200°F. Place the beef, thyme, Worcestershire sauce, and ¼ teaspoon salt in a bowl. Using the large holes on a box grater-shredder, shred the butter over the meat and gently mix until incorporated. Using your hands, divide the meat mixture into 8 equal portions and shape each portion into a 3-inch patty.

Place the rolls in the oven to warm. In a heavy frying pan over medium heat, cook the patties, turning once, until well browned, 2–3 minutes on each side for medium-rare, or until done to your liking. Remove from the heat.

Split the warm rolls in half horizontally and arrange the roll bases, cut side up, on a work surface. Top each base with a beef patty and then top with a dollop of the chutney. Cover with the roll tops, arrange on a warmed platter, and serve right away.

Smokiness is delivered to the chutney in two ways: by charring the tomato peels before puréeing them, and then adding a measure of smoked Spanish paprika. The resulting sweet-tart-smoky sauce contrasts nicely with miniature beef patties, made even richer and juicier by the addition of frozen butter before shaping.

salmon cakes with wasabi mayonnaise

This simple sauce made from intensely hot wasabi is tempered by sweet honey, tart lemon, and rich mayonnaise. It deliciously sets off the flavor of sea-fresh salmon, formed here into a twist on classic crab cakes with an Asian flair.

Flake the salmon into a bowl, removing any errant bones as you work. Add the onion, ½ cup of the bread crumbs, ¼ teaspoon salt, pepper to taste, and 1 tablespoon of the mayonnaise and mix gently. Add a little more mayonnaise if needed to bind the mixture.

Using your hands, form the mixture into 6 equal cakes about 3 inches in diameter. Place the cakes on a plate, cover, and refrigerate for about 15 minutes to blend the flavors and become firm.

Meanwhile, in a bowl, whisk together the ½ cup mayonnaise, 1 teaspoon wasabi, ½ teaspoon honey, and 1 teaspoon lemon juice. Season to taste with additional wasabi, honey, or lemon.

Pour the oil into a heavy 10-inch frying pan to a depth of ½ inch and place over high heat. While the oil is heating, place the flour, egg, and the remaining ½ cup bread crumbs in 3 separate bowls; lightly beat the egg.

One at a time, dip the salmon cakes in the flour, coating both sides and shaking off the excess. Next, coat the cakes with the egg, allowing the excess to drip off. Finally, coat the cakes with the bread crumbs, again shaking off the excess. Set the coated cakes on a plate as you work. Carefully add the coated cakes to the hot oil and fry until golden brown on the first sides, about 2 minutes. Using a slotted spatula, turn the cakes over and fry on the second sides until golden brown, about 2 minutes longer.

Transfer the cakes to warmed individual plates. Top each with a dollop of wasabi mayonnaise and serve right away.

cooked salmon, preferably wild king salmon, ½ pound

white onion, 1 tablespoon minced

panko bread crumbs, 1 cup

sea salt and freshly ground pepper

homemade mayonnaise (page 144), ½ cup plus about 1 tablespoon

wasabi paste, 1 teaspoon, or to taste

honey, ½ teaspoon, or to taste

fresh lemon juice, 1 teaspoon, or to taste

rice bran or canola oil for frying

all-purpose flour, ¼ cup

large egg, 1

MAKES 6 CAKES;
3 OR 6 SERVINGS

grilled fish skewers with cilantro and cumin

garlic, 2 cloves

fresh cilantro, ⅔ cup coarsely chopped and firmly packed

ground cumin, 2 teaspoons

hot smoked paprika, ½ teaspoon

cayenne pepper, pinch

mild extra-virgin olive oil, ⅓ cup

fresh lemon juice, 3 tablespoons

swordfish or mahimahi fillet, 1 pound

canola oil for grilling

sea salt

MAKES 14 SKEWERS; 6–8 SERVINGS

On a cutting board, mash the garlic cloves to a paste with the side of a heavy knife. In a blender or food processor, combine the garlic, cilantro, cumin, paprika, cayenne pepper, olive oil, and lemon juice and process until blended but not completely smooth. Set aside ¼ cup of the cilantro mixture. Pour the remaining mixture into a nonreactive bowl.

Cut the fish into 1-inch cubes, removing any errant bones. You should have 28 cubes. Add the cubes to the bowl with the marinade, turn to coat evenly, cover, and marinate at room temperature for 30 minutes. Meanwhile, soak fourteen 9-inch bamboo skewers in water to cover for 30 minutes.

Prepare a charcoal or gas grill for direct-heat grilling over high heat.

Drain the fish cubes, discarding the marinade, and drain the skewers. Thread 2 fish cubes onto each skewer. Brush the grill rack with canola oil, then grill the skewers over direct heat, turning once, until the fish is nicely browned and just cooked through when tested with a small sharp knife, about 2 minutes on each side.

Arrange the skewers on a warmed platter, sprinkle lightly with salt, and pour the reserved cilantro mixture over the top. Serve right away.

This dish features a potent mixture of smoky and spicy North African–style seasonings: cumin, smoked paprika, and cayenne pepper. Here, the heady mixture does double duty, as a marinade and a sauce for simple skewers of meaty grilled fish.

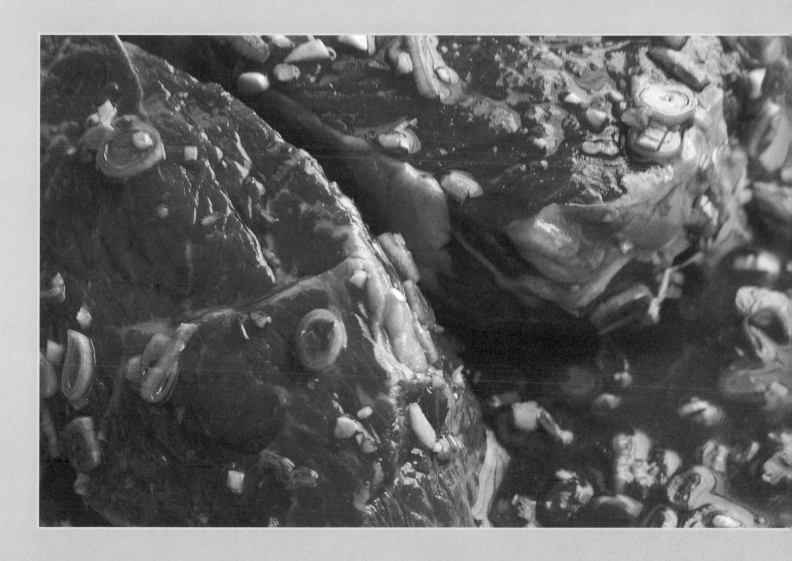

An Asian twist on beef tacos showcases the versatility of green onions. Their flavor is less pungent than mature onions, making them perfect for using both in marinades and sauces, as well as for flavorful and colorful garnishes.

lettuce tacos with grilled sesame beef

green onions, 4 large, white and pale green parts minced

garlic, 2 cloves, minced

soy sauce, ½ cup

mirin, 2 teaspoons

asian sesame oil, 1 teaspoon

red pepper flakes, ½–1 teaspoon

sirloin steak, 1 pound

sesame seeds, 1 tablespoon

butter or red leaf lettuce, 12 small cup-shaped leaves

MAKES 12 TACOS; 3–4 SERVINGS

In a shallow, nonreactive baking dish, combine half of the green onions, the garlic, soy sauce, mirin, sesame oil, and red pepper flakes. Add the steak and turn to coat evenly. Cover and refrigerate for at least 4 hours or for up to overnight, turning the steak from time to time.

Prepare a charcoal or gas grill for direct-heat grilling over high heat.

While the grill is heating, in a small, dry frying pan over medium heat, toast the sesame seeds, shaking the pan frequently, until pale gold and fragrant, 2–3 minutes. Pour onto a plate and let cool.

Remove the steak from the marinade and pat dry with paper towels. Place on the grill rack and cook, turning once, until well browned on both sides, about 4 minutes on each side for medium-rare, or until done to your liking. Transfer the steak to a cutting board and let rest for about 5 minutes.

Using a sharp knife, thinly slice the steak on the diagonal across the grain and then cut it crosswise into small pieces. Arrange the lettuce cups on a platter. Divide the steak among the cups, sprinkle with the sesame seeds and remaining green onions, and serve right away.

In this high-impact marinade, each of the six ingredients plays an important role. Based on a Korean-style recipe, it embodies the Asian technique of layering flavors—here, nutty sesame seeds and sesame oil combine with a host of salty, sweet, and spicy ingredients to create a dish that's complex in taste, but still simple in execution.

fall

mushroom tartlets with cornmeal crusts

**cornmeal tarlet dough
(page 144)**

unsalted butter,
2 tablespoons

shallot, ½, minced

garlic, 1 clove, minced

**mixed wild and cultivated
mushrooms,** ½ pound,
tough stems removed,
chopped

cream cheese, 2 ounces

**sea salt and freshly ground
pepper**

black truffle oil,
2 teaspoons

button mushrooms,
about 4

fresh chives, ¼ cup
chopped

MAKES 24 TARTLETS;
6–8 SERVINGS

Preheat the oven to 350°F. Have ready 1 or 2 miniature muffin pans with a total of 24 muffin cups.

Roll out 1 dough disk between sheets of waxed paper until ⅛ inch thick. Using a 3-inch round pastry cutter, cut out as many rounds as possible from the dough. Transfer the rounds to the muffin cups, pressing them in evenly. Using a fork, prick the bottom of each cup 2–3 times. Reserve the dough scraps. Repeat with the remaining dough disk. Gather all the dough scraps, pat them into a disk, roll it out ⅛ inch thick, and cut out more rounds. Push the rounds into muffin cups; you should have 24 tartlet shells in all. Bake the tartlet shells until crisp and golden, about 20 minutes. Transfer to a rack and let the shells cool completely in the pan.

In a large sauté pan over medium heat, melt the butter. Add the shallot and garlic and sauté until fragrant, about 1 minute. Add the chopped mixed mushrooms and cook until they begin to soften and the liquid they release evaporates, about 5 minutes. Add the cream cheese and season to taste with salt and pepper. Add the truffle oil and stir until the cream cheese melts. Remove from the heat, cover, and keep warm.

Trim the stem ends of the button mushrooms, and then thinly slice the mushrooms vertically. Heat a dry nonstick frying pan over low heat. Add the mushroom slices in a single layer and cook for about 30 seconds; the mushrooms will be barely cooked.

To serve, carefully remove the tartlet shells from the pans. Spoon the warm mushroom–cream cheese filling into the tartlet shells, dividing it evenly. Top each tartlet with 1 mushroom slice and a sprinkle of chives. Arrange on a warmed platter and serve right away.

The earthiness of the mushrooms in these small tarts is enhanced by the nuttiness of the cornmeal crusts, and reinforced by the potent, musky truffle oil in the creamy filling. Using a variety of fresh mushrooms, both wild and cultivated, gives these tartlets great texture and bold taste.

cheese-stuffed risotto cakes

Stuffed with smoked mozzarella cheese and then coated with crisp bread crumbs, these pleasingly rich, creamy textured rice cakes make a big flavor impact with little effort. Inside each crisp, golden brown cake is a smoky, oozy surprise for your guests.

Cut the cheese into 10 thin, 2-inch-square pieces. Scoop up ¼ cup of the cold risotto and shape it into ball between your palms. Make an indentation in the ball with a fingertip and press a piece of the cheese into the cavity. Bring the rice over the cheese to cover it completely, and then flatten the rice into a cake 3 inches in diameter and ½ inch thick. Repeat with the remaining risotto and cheese to make 10 cakes.

Preheat the oven to 200°F. Line a large baking sheet with paper towels and place a wire rack on top. Pour the oil into a large, heavy frying pan to a depth of ½ inch and warm over high heat until very hot.

While the oil is heating, place the flour, egg, and bread crumbs in 3 separate bowls; lightly beat the egg. One at a time, dip the risotto cakes in the flour, coating both sides and shaking off the excess. Next, coat both sides of the cakes with the egg, allowing the excess to drip off. Finally, coat the cakes with the bread crumbs, again shaking off the excess. Set the coated cakes aside on a plate as you work.

Working in batches to avoid crowding the pan, fry the coated cakes in the hot oil until golden brown and crisp on the first sides, about 2 minutes. Using a slotted spatula, turn the cakes over and fry on the second sides until golden brown, about 2 minutes longer. Transfer the cakes to the rack to drain and keep warm in the oven. Cook the remaining cakes in the same way, adding more oil to the pan as needed.

Arrange the cakes on a warmed platter and serve right away.

smoked mozzarella cheese, ¼ pound

leftover risotto or basic risotto (page 145), cold, 2½ cups

rice bran or canola oil for frying

all-purpose flour, ½ cup

large egg, 1

panko bread crumbs, 1 cup

MAKES 10 CAKES;
4–5 SERVINGS

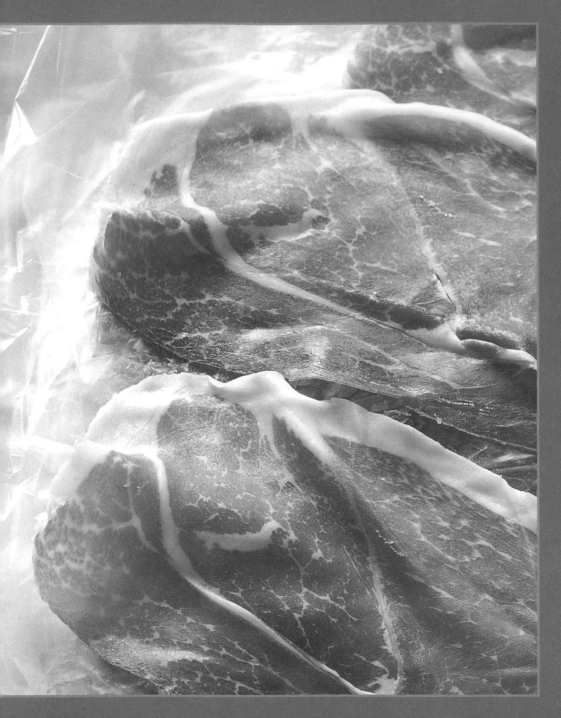

Prosciutto and figs are a classic hors d'oeuvre pairing. Here, they're enlivened by first cooking the fruits over a smoky grill to concentrate their natural sugars. They're then stuffed with bold blue cheese, which reinforces the contrast to the salty, meaty ham.

grilled figs with prosciutto and gorgonzola

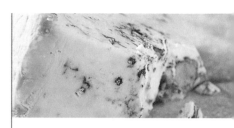

fresh mission figs,
16, firm but ripe

gorgonzola cheese,
piccante or *dolce,*
2 ounces

canola oil for grilling

prosciutto di parma,
16 paper-thin slices

**aged balsamic vinegar
for drizzling**

**extra-virgin olive oil
for drizzling**

MAKES 16 STUFFED FIGS;
8 SERVINGS

Prepare a charcoal or gas grill for direct-heat grilling over medium heat, or preheat a stove-top grill pan over medium heat.

Cut two 1-inch-long slits in the shape of an X across the top of each fig. Stuff each fig with about ½ teaspoon of the cheese and press the sides of the fig together to close.

Brush the grill rack with canola oil. Place the figs on their sides on the grill rack and cook until they begin to char, 2–3 minutes. Using tongs, carefully turn the figs over and continue cooking until the cheese begins to melt, about 2 minutes longer.

Transfer the figs to a platter. Fold each prosciutto slice and stuff inside, drape over, or wrap around a fig. Drizzle a little vinegar and oil over the tops of the figs and serve right away.

Assertive gorgonzola cheese is a sophisticated counterpoint to naturally sweet fresh figs, which gain a smoky undertone when cooked on an outdoor grill. Salty prosciutto and tart-sweet balsamic vinegar add more intriguing layers to this easy-to-assemble starter, which is best eaten with knife and fork.

dates stuffed with chorizo and goat cheese

Here is the perfect example of the concept of layering flavors: sweet dates, smoky, meaty Spanish chorizo, and tangy aged goat cheese combine to form an-easy-to-put-together appetizer with a surprisingly complex taste.

Using a small, sharp knife, cut a lengthwise slit in each date, from the top to the bottom, and remove the pit.

Pull off the casing from the chorizo. Cut the chorizo and cheese each into 30 thin strips that will fit inside the dates.

Insert a strip of chorizo and a strip of cheese into each date and press the slit closed. Arrange the dates on a platter. (The platter can be covered and left at room temperature for several hours before serving.) Serve the appetizers with or without toothpicks.

dates, preferably deglet noor, 30 small

hot spanish chorizo, ¼ pound

semifirm spanish goat's milk cheese, preferably *cabra al vino,* ¼ pound

MAKES 30 STUFFED DATES; 6–8 SERVINGS

Butternut squash blended with exotic seasonings is an inspired alternative to potatoes in fried, Indian-style samosas. A bold dipping sauce made from tart, fruity tamarind paste helps counter the natural sweetness of the vegetable.

curried butternut squash samosas with tamarind chutney

Here, vibrant curry powder is combined with pungent garlic and piquant onions to become a zesty foil for creamy butternut squash. A crisp wonton shell counters the resulting sweet-spicy filling, then the little filled pastries are offset by a pleasantly tart tamarind-based sauce.

Preheat the oven to 400°F. Cut the squash in half lengthwise and scoop out and discard the seeds. Place the halves, cut sides up, on a rimmed baking sheet and drizzle with 1 tablespoon of the olive oil. Bake the squash until tender when pierced with a knife, about 40 minutes. Let cool until easy to handle. Scoop the cooled squash flesh into a bowl and discard the shells.

In a saucepan over medium-low heat, warm the remaining 2 tablespoons olive oil. Add the onion and garlic and sauté until the onion is soft, about 5 minutes. Remove from the heat and stir in the curry powder. Add the squash flesh and mash with a potato masher until almost smooth. Stir in the salt and sugar, then taste and adjust the seasonings.

In a small bowl, beat the egg with a fork until blended. Lay about 5 wonton wrappers on a work surface; keep the remaining wrappers covered with a slightly damp kitchen towel. Spoon a scant tablespoon of the squash filling in the center of each wrapper and flatten with the bottom of the spoon. Brush the edges of the wrapper with the egg. Fold each wrapper in half on the diagonal, forming a triangle, then press the edges together to seal the filling inside; set aside. Repeat with the remaining wrappers and filling.

Preheat the oven to 200°F. Line a large baking sheet with paper towels and place a wire rack on top. Pour canola oil into a heavy, high-sided skillet to a depth of 3 inches and warm over medium-high heat until very hot. Working in batches, add the samosas to the oil and fry, turning once, until golden brown on both sides, about 2 minutes on each side. Using a slotted spoon, transfer the samosas to the rack to drain and keep warm in the oven. Cook the remaining samosas in the same way, adding oil to the pan as needed.

Arrange the samosas on a warmed platter and set the chutney alongside for dipping. Serve right away.

butternut squash, 1 (about 1½ pounds)

olive oil, 3 tablespoons

white onion, 2 tablespoons chopped

garlic, 2 cloves, chopped

madras curry powder, 1 tablespoon

sea salt, 1 teaspoon

sugar, 1 teaspoon

large egg, 1

square wonton wrappers, 1 package (1 pound)

canola or rice bran oil for deep-frying

tamarind chutney (page 144)

MAKES 40 SAMOSAS; 8–10 SERVINGS

chickpea dip with toasted cumin and pomegranate

cumin seeds, 1 teaspoon

garlic, 2 cloves

sea salt

lemons, 2

chickpeas, 2 cans
(15 ounces each)

pomegranate, 1

fruity extra-virgin olive oil,
¼ cup, plus oil for drizzling

**cumin-crusted pita chips
(page 144) or baguette
slices for serving**

MAKES 8–10 SERVINGS

In a small, dry frying pan over medium heat, toast the cumin seeds, shaking the pan often, until fragrant, about 2 minutes. Pour onto a plate to cool.

In a mortar, combine the garlic and a pinch of salt and crush to a paste with a pestle. Add the toasted cumin seeds and grind them together with the garlic. Grate enough zest from 1 lemon to measure ½ teaspoon, and then halve and juice both lemons. Drain the chickpeas, rinse under cold running water, and drain well again.

Score the pomegranate into quarters with a sharp knife and pull the fruit apart into sections. Place the sections in a bowl and add water to cover. Using your fingers, pry the seeds away from the membranes; the seeds will sink to the bottom the bowl, while the membrane and skin will float to the top. Scoop out and discard the membrane and skin, and then drain the seeds and set aside.

In a food processor or blender, combine the chickpeas, garlic-cumin mixture, lemon zest, 4 tablespoons lemon juice, ¼ cup olive oil, and ¼ cup water. Process the mixture until very creamy, adding more water if needed to achieve the desired consistency. Season to taste with salt and lemon juice.

Scrape the dip onto a large plate. Drizzle with olive oil and sprinkle with about ½ cup pomegranate seeds (reserve any remaining seeds for another use or for snacking). Serve with the pita chips.

Pomegranate seeds lend an extra layer of tart-sweet flavor as well as an appealing crunch to this creamy dip, a modern twist on hummus. The unique taste of cumin seeds is released when they are toasted, delivering a pleasant smokiness to the dish.

oysters on the half shell with apple-horseradish slaw

Plump, briny, Atlantic oysters are cleverly offset by tangy green apple and pungent horseradish in the crunchy slaw that tops them here. A small amount of crème fraîche mellows the assertiveness of the topping, and its richness matches that of the oysters.

Scrub the shell of each oyster with a stiff-bristled brush and rinse thoroughly under cold running water. Discard any oysters that do not close when touched.

To shuck each oyster, grip it, flat side up, with a folded kitchen towel (to protect your hand). Positioning an oyster knife to one side of the hinge (opposite the shell's concentric ridges), push the tip between the shells and pry upward to open. Keeping the blade firmly against the top shell, run it around the perimeter of the oyster to sever the muscle holding the shell halves together. Discard the top shells. Run the knife underneath the oyster to free it from the bottom shell, being careful not to spill the juice, or "liquor," and then set the oyster in its shell on a plate. Repeat with the remaining oysters. Refrigerate the oysters until ready to serve.

Peel, quarter, and core the apple. Using a mandoline or a large, sharp chef's knife, slice the apple quarters paper-thin. A few at a time, stack the slices and cut them into thin julienne. Cut the celery into thin julienne less than 1 inch long. In a bowl, combine the apple, celery, horseradish, and crème fraîche and mix gently until well combined.

When ready to serve, pour a thin layer of coarse salt onto a platter. Arrange the oysters on top of the salt, taking care not to spill the juice. Spoon an equal amount of the apple-horseradish slaw on top of each oyster and serve right away; provide small shellfish forks, if desired.

atlantic oysters, such as malapeque, 12

granny smith apple, 1

celery, 1 stalk

prepared horseradish, 1 teaspoon

crème fraîche (page 144 or purchased), 2 teaspoons

coarse salt for serving

MAKES 4–6 SERVINGS

steamed buns with roast duck and dried cherry sauce

all-purpose flour, 2¼ cups

sugar, ¾ cup

baking powder,
3½ teaspoons

kosher salt, ½ teaspoon

whole milk, ⅓ cup

peanut oil, 3 tablespoons

dried cherries, 1 cup

five-spice powder,
¼ teaspoon

fruity, robust red wine,
such as zinfandel, 1 cup

soy sauce, 1 tablespoon

cornstarch, 2 tablespoons

chinese-style roast duck, 1

green onion tops, finely
slivered, for garnish

MAKES 8–10 SERVINGS

In a bowl, mix the flour, ½ cup of the sugar, the baking powder, and salt. Add the milk, oil, and 3 tablespoons water and stir until a dough forms. Cover with a damp towel and set aside at room temperature for 1 hour.

In a small saucepan, combine the cherries, the remaining ¼ cup sugar, the five-spice powder, wine, soy sauce, and 2 cups water. Bring to a boil over high heat, and then reduce the heat to low and simmer, stirring occasionally, until the mixture is slightly thickened and reduced to about 2 cups, about 20 minutes. Dissolve the cornstarch in ¼ cup water. Add it to the pan and simmer, stirring, until thickened, about 1 minute. Let cool completely. Pour into a serving bowl, cover, and set aside.

Have ready 2 bamboo steamers and a wok. On a lightly floured work surface, knead the dough until smooth and elastic, about 10 minutes. Divide the dough into 16 equal pieces. Roll 1 piece into a ball, and then flatten the ball into a 3-inch disk and place on a steamer tray. Repeat with the remaining dough pieces, spacing them at least 3 inches apart.

Bring 2 inches of water to a boil in the wok. Stack the bamboo steamers over the water, cover, and steam the buns gently until light and fluffy and cooked through, 10–15 minutes. Do not overcook.

Preheat the oven to 200°F. While the buns are steaming, use a knife to cut the duck meat off the carcass into bite-sized pieces, leaving the crisp skin attached. Arrange the duck pieces on a platter and cover with aluminum foil. Put the platter in the oven to slightly warm the duck.

When the buns are ready, transfer them to warmed plates. Top each with a few pieces of duck, a spoonful of the cherry sauce, and a few green onion slivers. Serve right away.

Sweet-tart dried cherries are a classic partner to duck, as they help cut through the richness of the meat. Here, they're made into a sauce with robust red wine and salt-tinged soy sauce. Steamy hot buns are the perfect foil for the savory duck and fruity sauce, creating a conversation-sparking appetizer or small plate.

Smoked trout is an intriguing stand-in for more assertive smoked salmon. Fresh dill and chives, blended with tangy crème fraîche, cleverly offset its bold flavor as well as the sweetness of the crisp sweet potato pancakes that the trout adorns.

sweet potato cakes with smoked trout and herbed crème fraîche

lemon, 1

crème fraîche (page 144 or purchased), ½ cup

fresh dill, 1½ teaspoons minced

fresh chives, 1 teaspoon minced

sweet potato, 1 (about 8 ounces)

russet potato, 1 (about 8 ounces)

sea salt

large eggs, 2

all-purpose flour, ⅓ cup

freshly ground pepper, pinch

rice bran or canola oil, ½ cup

hot-smoked trout fillet, ¼ pound

MAKES 15 CAKES;
3–4 SERVINGS

Grate the zest from the lemon, then halve and juice the fruit. In a bowl, combine the crème fraîche, dill, chives, and the lemon zest and juice and mix well. Refrigerate until serving.

Peel the sweet potato and russet potato. Using the large holes on a box grater-shredder, shred the potatoes into a bowl. Add 1 teaspoon salt and toss well. Let stand for 10 minutes, then transfer to a sieve, rinse under cold running water, and drain well. Return the potatoes to the bowl.

In a small bowl, whisk the eggs until blended, and then add to the potatoes along with the flour, ½ teaspoon salt, and the pepper and mix well.

Preheat the oven to 200°F. Line a large baking sheet with paper towels and place a wire rack on top. Pour the oil into a deep, heavy 12-inch frying pan and warm over medium-high heat until hot but not smoking. Spoon a heaping tablespoon of the potato mixture into the hot oil and, using a slotted spatula, flatten it into a cake about 3 inches in diameter. Repeat to form 4 more cakes, spacing them well apart. Fry, turning once, until golden on both sides, about 3 minutes total. Using the spatula, transfer the pancakes to the wire rack to drain and keep warm in the oven. Repeat with the remaining potato mixture in 2 batches.

To serve, use your fingers to break the trout into large flakes. Arrange the pancakes on a large warmed platter. Top each pancake with a piece of trout and a dollop of the herbed crème fraîche. Serve right away.

Traditional potato pancakes are given a surprising twist with the addition of sweet potato to the batter. The root vegetable's slight sugariness forms a pleasing contrast to smoked trout and a tangy topping of fresh herb–spiked crème fraîche.

savory apple, cheddar, and thyme turnovers

These turnovers combine two classic partners— tart apple and nutty cheddar cheese—in a rich puff pastry cloak. The addition of fresh thyme, and the absence of sugar, turns these triangular puffs into a savory appetizer instead of the more expected dessert.

Preheat the oven to 400°F. Peel, quarter, and core the apple. Thinly slice the quarters and then cut into small dice.

Have ready a small bowl of water. In a small saucepan, melt the butter over low heat, and set the pan next to the water near your work surface.

Roll out each sheet of puff pastry until it measures about 10 by 12 inches. Cut each sheet of pastry into 12 almost-square pieces. Top each piece with ½ teaspoon of the cheese, 1 teaspoon of the apple, and a small amount of thyme. Brush the edges of the pastry pieces with the water, then fold each piece in half on the diagonal to form a triangle. Press the edges together to seal. Place the turnovers on a baking sheet, spacing them about ½ inch apart. Brush the tops with the butter and sprinkle with the remaining cheese.

Bake the turnovers until golden brown, about 15 minutes. Transfer to a warmed platter and serve right away.

tart apple, such as granny smith, 1

unsalted butter, about 4 tablespoons

frozen all-butter puff pastry, 2 sheets, each about 9 inches square, thawed according to package directions

aged farmhouse cheddar cheese, 1 cup shredded

fresh thyme, 1 tablespoon chopped

MAKES 24 TURNOVERS; 6–8 SERVINGS

Make the most of the highly anticipated fall mushroom season by featuring them in a simple salad. The drippings from cooked smoked bacon replace most of the oil in the pungent, warm vinaigrette that dresses the fungi among a tangle of sturdy lettuces.

warm **wild mushroom** salad
with **bacon** vinaigrette

*A simple vinaigrette made
from nutty Spanish sherry
vinegar and salty-smoky
bacon enhances an earthy
mixture of mushrooms
in this autumnal salad.
Bitter radicchio and
peppery arugula are layered
with the warm mushroom
mixture for extra flavor,
color, and crunch.*

Trim the base of the mushroom stems, then thickly slice the mushrooms.

In a large frying pan over medium heat, melt the butter. Add about two-thirds of the shallots and sauté until translucent, about 5 minutes. Add the mushrooms and sauté until tender and the moisture they release evaporates, about 6 minutes.

Meanwhile, in another large frying pan over medium-high heat, cook the bacon, stirring occasionally, until browned and crisp, about 6 minutes. Remove from the heat and stir in the remaining shallots, the olive oil, vinegar, and mustard. Keep warm.

Transfer the mushrooms to a large bowl, add the bacon mixture, and toss to mix. Season to taste with salt and pepper. Add the radicchio and arugula and toss to coat the leaves well with the dressing.

Immediately arrange the salad on a large platter or divide it among individual plates and serve right away.

**mixed wild and cultivated
mushrooms,** 1 pound,
tough stems removed

unsalted butter,
1 tablespoon

shallots, 3, minced

bacon, preferably apple-wood smoked or berkshire,
2 slices, cut crosswise into
¼ inch pieces

extra-virgin olive oil,
2 tablespoons

sherry vinegar,
2 tablespoons

whole-grain mustard,
1 tablespoon

**sea salt and freshly ground
pepper**

radicchio leaves, from
1 head

arugula leaves, ½ bunch

MAKES 4 SERVINGS

winter

filo rolls with arugula, spinach, and feta

arugula, 2 bunches (about ½ pound), tough stems removed

spinach, 1 small bunch (about ½ pound), tough stems removed

feta cheese, preferably greek, ½ pound

unsalted butter, ¾ cup

filo dough, 14 sheets, each 13 by 17 inches

MAKES 42 PASTRIES; 10–12 SERVINGS

Preheat the oven to 350°F. Line a rimmed baking sheet with parchment paper. Rinse the arugula and spinach thoroughly and place in a large, heavy saucepan with the rinsing water still clinging to the leaves. Place over medium-high heat, cover, and cook, stirring occasionally, until wilted, 3–5 minutes. Remove from the heat, transfer to a sieve, and press the greens with a wooden spoon to drain well.

Finely chop the greens and place in a bowl. Crumble the cheese into the bowl with the greens and mix gently. In a small saucepan over low heat, melt the butter and pour into a bowl. Place the stack of filo sheets near the work surface and keep the sheets covered with a barely damp kitchen towel to prevent them from drying out when not using them.

Remove 1 filo sheet from the stack, lay it on the work surface, and brush lightly with the butter. Top with a second sheet and brush lightly with butter. Cut the stacked sheets lengthwise into 6 equal strips. Spoon a scant teaspoon of the filling near the end of 1 strip closest to you. Roll the edge over the filling, fold over ¼ inch of both sides of the strip, and then roll up the filling into a tight cylinder. Place the cylinders on a rimmed baking sheet and brush lightly with butter. Repeat with the remaining strips and then the remaining filo sheets until all of the filling and sheets have been used.

Bake the cylinders until golden brown, about 25 minutes. Transfer to a wire rack and let cool slightly on the pan.

Arrange the filo rolls on 1 or 2 warmed platters and serve right away.

Earthy spinach and salty feta cheese are traditional partners in Greek cuisine. Here, they're pumped up with peppery arugula in these crunchy, butter-rich miniature pastries that are a variation on traditional spanakopita.

bitter greens salad with spiced pecans and persimmons

Buttery pecans coated with a smoky-hot spice mixture accent the bitter winter lettuces in this salad. Sweet, yet pleasantly astringent persimmons provide a refreshing counterpoint. Salty and nutty Parmigiano tops off the dish simply with its unique savory taste.

To make the spiced pecans, in a heavy frying pan over medium heat, melt the butter. Add the cumin, cinnamon, and cayenne and stir until aromatic, about 30 seconds. Add the vanilla and a scant ¼ teaspoon salt, stir well, and then add the pecans. Cook the pecans, stirring often, until lightly toasted, about 3 minutes. Using a slotted spoon, transfer to paper towels to drain. Let the nuts cool completely.

Cut the persimmons in half lengthwise, trim off the stem ends and cut the halves into thin slices.

In a small bowl, whisk together the vinegar, olive oil, and mayonnaise until well blended to make a dressing. Season to taste with salt and pepper.

Place the salad greens in a bowl, drizzle with the dressing, and toss to coat evenly. Add the persimmons and spiced pecans to the bowl. Using a vegetable peeler, shave curls of the cheese into the bowl and toss gently. Divide the salad among chilled plates and serve right away.

unsalted butter, 2 tablespoons

ground cumin, ¼ teaspoon

ground cinnamon, ¼ teaspoon

cayenne pepper, pinch

vanilla extract, ½ teaspoon

sea salt and freshly ground black pepper

pecan halves, 1 cup

fuyu persimmons, 4

champagne vinegar, 2 tablespoons

extra-virgin olive oil, ⅓ cup

homemade mayonnaise (page 144), 2 tablespoons

mixed bitter salad greens, such as radicchio, arugula, escarole, and frisée, ¼ pound

parmigiano-reggiano cheese, 3 ounces, at room temperature

MAKES 8 SERVINGS

Prepare an upscale version of stuffed peppers by using imported piquillo peppers as a colorful, piquant shell. Dungeness crabmeat, in season beginning in December, adds another layer of elegance as the base for a flavorful filling.

crab-stuffed piquillo peppers

Fleshy, lightly spicy piquillo peppers are the perfect vehicle for a garlic-spiked crabmeat and potato filling. This sophisticated starter is deceptively easy to make, and the layered flavors will impress your guests with their complexity.

Preheat the oven to 425°F. Prick the skin of the potato in a few places with a fork. Place the potato in a small, shallow pan and bake until tender when pierced with a knife, about 1 hour. Let the potato cool until it can be handled. Reduce the oven temperature to 350°F.

Cut the potato in half lengthwise and scoop the flesh into a bowl. In a mortar, combine the garlic and salt and mash to a paste with a pestle. Add 2 tablespoons olive oil and mix well. Transfer the mixture to the bowl with the potato flesh and mix well. Pick over the crabmeat for shell fragments, and then fold it into the potato mixture until evenly distributed.

Oil a baking dish large enough to hold the peppers in a single layer. Drain the peppers well. Using a long, slender spoon, and being careful not to tear the peppers, gently stuff the potato-crabmeat mixture into the peppers, dividing it evenly. Place the stuffed peppers in the prepared baking dish and drizzle lightly with olive oil.

Bake the peppers just until the filling is heated through, about 5 minutes. Transfer the peppers to warmed individual plates and serve right away.

russet potato, 1 (about 8 ounces)

garlic, 1 clove

sea salt, ¼ teaspoon

fruity extra-virgin olive oil

fresh-cooked crabmeat, such as dungeness, ¼ pound

***piquillo* peppers,** 1 jar (12 ounces)

MAKES 6 SERVINGS

spiced lamb meatballs with garlicky yogurt sauce

plain yogurt, 1 cup

garlic, 1 clove, minced

nonstick cooking spray

firm white sandwich bread, 2 slices

ground lamb, preferably grass fed, 1 pound

green onions, 3, white and pale green parts thinly sliced

fresh flat-leaf parsley, ¼ cup minced

large egg, 1

ground cumin, 1 teaspoon

sweet paprika, 1 teaspoon

freshly ground pepper, 1 teaspoon

ground allspice, ¼ teaspoon

sea salt, 1½ teaspoons

MAKES ABOUT 40 MEAT-BALLS; 8–10 SERVINGS

In a small serving bowl, stir together the yogurt and garlic until well blended. Set aside at room temperature until serving.

Preheat the oven to 400°F. Line a rimmed baking sheet with aluminum foil and spray the foil with cooking spray.

Remove the crusts from the bread slices, and then tear the slices into small pieces and place in a bowl. Sprinkle 2 tablespoons water over the bread slices and toss to moisten evenly.

In another bowl, add the lamb, green onions, most of the parsley (save a small amount to garnish the sauce), the egg, cumin, paprika, pepper, allspice, and salt and mix together gently with your hands. Scoop up a heaping teaspoon of the mixture, shape into a ball between your palms, and place on the prepared baking sheet. Repeat to shape the remaining mixture; you should have about 40 meatballs total.

Bake the meatballs until browned and cooked through, about 15 minutes.

Transfer the meatballs to a warmed platter and place the sauce alongside for dipping. Serve right away with cocktail picks for spearing.

The creamy, mildly tangy taste of this yogurt-based dipping sauce counteracts the natural richness of the lamb. It also helps temper the boldly spiced meatballs, which are infused with a variety of zesty North African seasonings.

An original take on individual pizzas matches highly spiced lamb sausage with pleasantly bitter broccoli rabe for a Mediterranean-inspired appetizer. A hearty crust made from whole-wheat flour stands up to the bold flavors of the toppings.

whole-wheat pizzette with lamb, broccoli rabe, and olives

whole-wheat pizza dough (page 145), 1 ball, or about 1 pound purchased dough

cornmeal

olive oil

broccoli rabe, ½ small bunch

fresh lamb sausage, such as *merguez,* ½ pound

fontina val d'aosta cheese, 6 ounces, finely shredded

gaeta olives, 8, pitted and sliced

MAKES 16 PIZZETTE;
6–8 SERVINGS

Divide the dough into 16 equal balls. With oiled fingers, press each ball out into a 2- to 3-inch round. Cover the rounds with a clean kitchen towel and let stand for 10 minutes to rise slightly. Meanwhile, preheat the oven to 450°F. Dust 2 large rimmed baking sheets with cornmeal.

Bring a saucepan three-fourths full of water to a boil over high heat. Cut off the tough stem ends (about 1 inch) from the broccoli rabe, and then chop the rest into small pieces. Add the broccoli rabe to the boiling water and boil until tender, about 7 minutes. Drain into a colander and rinse under cold running water. Drain again and pat dry.

In a frying pan over medium heat, warm a small amount of olive oil. Remove the sausage from its casing and crumble the meat into the pan. Sauté, breaking up any sausage lumps with a wooden spoon, until browned, about 5 minutes. Remove from the heat and set aside.

Arrange 8 dough rounds on each prepared baking sheet, spacing them evenly. Top each dough round with an equal amount of the cheese, broccoli rabe, sausage, and olive pieces. Bake until the crusts are golden brown, the cheese melts, and the toppings are hot, 8–10 minutes.

Transfer the pizzette to a warmed serving platter and serve right away.

Peppery, mildly bitter broccoli rabe pairs with assertive lamb sausage and salty black Gaeta olives in these creative starter-sized pizzas. Nutty whole-wheat pizza dough contributes to the heartiness of the dish, while rich fontina cheese helps bring all the flavors into balance.

lobster, avocado, and grapefruit cocktail

Sweet lobster meat needs little to enhance its unique taste. Here, bracing grapefruit and nutty, rich avocado set it off nicely. A simple dressing of fresh lemon, fruity olive oil, and oniony chives helps the ingredients shine without masking their individual attributes.

Cut or tear the lobster into small bite-sized pieces. Halve, pit, and peel the avocado, and then cut into small bite-sized chunks.

Cut a thin slice off the blossom and stem end of the grapefruit to reveal the flesh. Stand the grapefruit upright and cut off the peel and pith in thick strips, cutting from top to bottom and following the curve of the fruit. Holding the grapefruit over a bowl, cut along both sides of each section to free it from the membrane, allowing the sections to drop into the bowl. Cut each section in half, if desired.

In a small bowl, whisk together the olive oil, lemon juice, and chives to make a dressing. Season to taste with salt.

Add the lobster and avocado to the bowl with the grapefruit. Drizzle with the dressing and toss to coat evenly. Divide evenly among 4 small cocktail glasses. Serve right away.

freshly cooked lobster meat, ¼ pound

hass avocado, 1

red grapefruit, preferably texas, 1 large

mild extra-virgin olive oil, 1 tablespoon

fresh lemon juice, 1 teaspoon

fresh chives, 1 tablespoon minced

sea salt

MAKES 4 SERVINGS

crostini with white beans, garlic, and tuscan kale

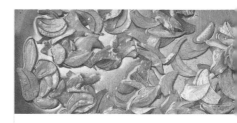

tuscan kale, 12 small leaves (about ¼ pound total weight)

peppery extra-virgin olive oil, 2 tablespoons, plus oil for drizzling

garlic, 1 clove, thinly sliced

low-sodium chicken broth, ½ cup

baguette, 1

canned cannellini beans, 1½ cups, rinsed and drained

red pepper flakes

sea salt

MAKES 14 CROSTINI;
3–4 SERVINGS

Preheat the oven to 400°F.

Cut away and discard the central rib from each kale leaf and chop the leaves coarsely. In a large frying pan over high heat, warm the olive oil. Add the kale leaves and cook, stirring often, until they wilt and sizzle in the hot oil, about 2 minutes. Reduce the heat to medium-low, add the garlic and broth, cover, and cook until the leaves are tender but still hold their shape, about 10 minutes.

Meanwhile, cut the baguette on the diagonal into 14 slices, each ½ inch thick. (Reserve the remainder for another use.) Arrange the slices on a rimmed baking sheet and toast in the oven until crisp, turning them once, about 5 minutes total. Remove from the oven and set aside.

When the kale leaves are tender, push them to one side of the pan and add the beans to the other side. Season to taste with red pepper flakes and salt and simmer until the broth is mostly absorbed, about 5 minutes. Using a fork, stir together the beans and greens and roughly mash until the mixture just holds together. Season to taste with salt and red pepper flakes.

Spoon a heaping tablespoon of the beans and greens mixture on top of each toast and drizzle with olive oil. Arrange on a platter or individual plates and serve right away.

Pungent garlic, mellowed by braising, creamy white beans, and peppery olive oil combine to create an innovative topping for toasted bread slices. It's an inspired way to showcase the hearty, slightly bitter greens that proliferate in the winter farmers' market.

Undeniably pungent horseradish root, grated and mixed with cooling sour cream, makes a bold statement as a topping for cured salmon. Perched atop tiny buckwheat pancakes, the lox stars in a new twist on the blini-and-caviar theme.

buckwheat blini with lox and horseradish cream

unsalted butter,
2 tablespoons, plus butter for cooking blini

large egg, 1

plain yogurt, ¼ cup

whole milk, ⅓ cup

all-purpose flour, ⅓ cup

buckwheat flour, ¼ cup

sea salt

baking soda, ¼ teaspoon

sour cream, ½ cup

horseradish root,
½–1 teaspoon grated, or 1 teaspoon prepared horseradish

fresh lemon juice,
¼ teaspoon

thinly sliced lox, 6 ounces

small fresh dill sprigs for garnish

MAKES 14 BLINI;
3–4 SERVINGS

In a small saucepan, melt the 2 tablespoons butter and let cool. In a bowl, whisk together the egg, yogurt, and milk. In a small bowl, whisk together the all-purpose flour, buckwheat flour, a scant ¼ teaspoon salt, and the baking soda. Add the flour mixture to the egg mixture and whisk to mix. Add the cooled butter and whisk until a thick, lump-free batter forms.

In the small saucepan, over low heat, melt a few more tablespoons of butter. Heat a large nonstick frying pan or griddle over medium heat until hot, then brush the pan with some of the melted butter. Working in batches, add the batter to the pan by tablespoonfuls, spacing each portion well apart. Cook until slightly bubbly around the edges and the first sides are golden brown, about 1½ minutes. Turn the blini over and cook until the second sides are golden brown, about 30 seconds longer. Transfer to a plate and repeat with the remaining batter, adding more melted butter to the pan as needed to prevent sticking. You should have 14 blini, each about 3 inches in diameter.

In a small bowl, stir together the sour cream, ½ teaspoon grated horseradish, lemon juice, and salt to taste until blended. Add more horseradish if you prefer a bolder flavor.

Tear the lox into small pieces. Arrange the blini on a platter, then top each with a few pieces of salmon, a dollop of the horseradish cream, and a small sprig of dill. Serve right away.

Buckwheat flour has a strong malty, earthy flavor. Used to make tiny pancakes, its distinctive taste pairs well with silky cured salmon. Pungent horseradish and tangy fresh dill are classic partners for the fish, and here they help offset the rich sour cream topping that guilds the appetizers.

truffled fonduta with winter vegetables

Fontina Val d'Aosta, a cow's milk cheese with a mild nuttiness, develops a subtle earthy, woodsy bouquet when melted, which pairs well with the potent flavor of truffle oil. Melted together and enriched by butter and egg yolks, the ingredients become an indulgent topping for seasonal vegetables and toasted bread cubes.

Add the cheese to a small bowl. Pour in the cream and let stand at room temperature for 2 hours.

Bring 1–2 inches of water to a boil in a large saucepan. Cut the potatoes in half lengthwise. Arrange the broccoli, cauliflower, and potatoes in a collapsible steamer basket, place over (not touching) the water, cover, and steam until the broccoli and cauliflower are tender-crisp and the potatoes are cooked through, about 10 minutes. Set aside at room temperature.

Pour water to a depth of 1 inch in another saucepan and bring to a simmer over low heat. Put the butter in a heatproof bowl and place over (not touching) the water. Heat just until the butter softens and begins to melt. Increase the heat to medium and gently whisk in the cheese mixture 1 tablespoon at a time. When all of the cheese mixture has been added and the cheese has melted, remove the bowl from the pan, place on a work surface, and whisk in the egg yolks, one at time. Transfer the mixture to a blender and process until the mixture is thick and well blended.

Immediately divide the *fonduta* evenly among individual ramekins and drizzle a little truffle oil on top of each portion. Divide the vegetables and bread cubes among individual plates and place a ramekin of the *fonduta* on each plate. Or, spoon the *fonduta* over the vegetables, dividing it evenly, and drizzle with the truffle oil. Serve right away.

fontina val d'aosta cheese, ½ pound, shredded

heavy cream, 1 cup

fingerling potatoes, about 12 ounces

broccoli florets, 1 cup bite-sized

cauliflower florets, 1 cup bite-sized

unsalted butter, 4 tablespoons

large egg yolks, 2

white truffle oil, 1–2 teaspoons

baguette, 1, cut into ½-inch cubes

MAKES 4 SERVINGS

fried squid with smoked paprika aioli

homemade mayonnaise (page 144), ¾ cup

garlic, 1 clove, minced

spanish smoked paprika, 1 teaspoon, or to taste

sea salt

squid bodies and tentacles, 1 pound, cleaned

rice bran or canola oil for deep-frying

yellow cornmeal, ½ cup

semolina flour, ½ cup

MAKES 6 SERVINGS

In a bowl, combine the mayonnaise, garlic, and smoked paprika and mix well. Season to taste with salt and paprika. Refrigerate until ready to serve.

Cut the squid bodies into rings about ⅓ inch wide, drain well, and set aside along with the tentacles.

Pour oil into a heavy saucepan to a depth of 3 inches and warm over medium-high heat until it reaches 360°F on a deep-frying thermometer. Line a rimmed baking sheet with paper towels and place near the stove. Preheat the oven to 200°F.

While the oil is heating, in a bowl, combine the cornmeal, semolina, and 1½ teaspoons salt. Add the squid and toss until evenly coated. Using your hands, lift the squid out of the bowl, shaking off the excess, and place it on plate near the stove.

When the oil is ready, drop in about one-fourth of the coated squid and cook until golden brown and crisp, 1–2 minutes. Using a skimmer, transfer the squid to the paper towel–lined pan and keep warm in the oven. Repeat to fry the remaining squid.

Transfer the squid to a warmed platter and set the aioli alongside for dipping. Serve right away.

The bold flavor of smoked paprika is brought even more to the forefront when paired with some type of oil or fat, here the olive oil and egg yolk in the rich mayonnaise-based dipping sauce. It's enhanced by a generous dose of garlic, then served as a companion to crunchy cornmeal-coated fried squid.

An intriguing interplay of flavors, textures, and colors, this salad pairs crunchy hazelnuts, tart blood oranges, and crisp fennel in a dish reminiscent of those found in Turkish cafés. It's a novel way to showcase winter's prized citrus fruit.

blood orange salad with shaved fennel and hazelnuts

blood oranges, 4

fennel, 1 bulb

hazelnuts, ⅓–½ cup

hazelnut oil, about ⅓ cup

sea salt

MAKES 4 SERVINGS

Cut a thin slice off the blossom and stem end of 1 orange to reveal the flesh. Stand the orange upright and slice off the peel and pith in thick strips, cutting from top to bottom and following the curve of the fruit. Cut the orange crosswise into 1½ inch slices and remove any seeds from the slices with the tip of a knife. Repeat with the remaining oranges.

If the fennel stalks are still attached, trim them off and reserve for another use or discard. Reserve a few of the feathery fronds for garnish. Remove and discard the outer layer of the bulb if it is tough, or cut away any discolored areas. Halve the bulb lengthwise and trim the base of the core. Using a mandoline or sharp knife, cut the fennel bulb halves into paper-thin slices; you should have about 1 cup sliced fennel. Set aside.

In a small, dry frying pan over medium-low heat, toast the hazelnuts, stirring often, until lightly browned and fragrant, 4–6 minutes. Pour onto a plate to cool. Rub the hazelnuts in a clean kitchen towel to remove the skins and then coarsley chop.

Arrange the blood orange slices on a platter or individual plates. Top with the fennel slices, and then with the chopped nuts. Liberally drizzle each salad with hazelnut oil, sprinkle lightly with salt, and then garnish with small pieces of the fennel fronds. Serve right away.

Deeply nutty hazelnuts along with their assertive oil enhance a simple salad of sweet-sour blood oranges and anise-scented fennel. Served together, the few ingredients combine to make a first-course salad that's as beautiful as it is delicious.

fundamentals

The following pages offer some basic information on preparing and serving appetizers. Next are staple recipes for sauces, doughs, and accompaniments that are called for in this book, but which are also useful additions to any cook's repertory. The tips that follow show how to work with popular ingredients such as leeks, fresh herbs, and squid, and reveal key techniques like setting up a charcoal grill.

planning your meal

When you are planning a meal that includes an appetizer, odds are it is either a special family meal or you are expecting guests. A helpful initial step in planning your event is to ask yourself two questions: First, what type of event are you conceiving? Second, what is fresh and in season right now at the market? Your answers to these will help you refine the menu so you can start planning.

casual gathering If you are just seeking an appetizer to set out while you are serving drinks, consider attractive bowls of dips and accompaniments, or nibbles that you can serve at room temperature. In summer, try Avocado, Toasted Corn, and Chipotle Salsa (page 50), or, in fall, Chickpea Dip with Toasted Cumin and Pomegranate (page 95). Fava Bean and Ricotta Crostini with Fresh Mint (page 17) is ideal for a spring get-together. Crostini with White Beans, Garlic, and Tuscan Kale (page 129) is perfect for a wintertime party.

cocktail party Cocktail parties typically feature a selection of small finger foods and drinks, but not enough food to be considered dinner. If this is the type of party you have in mind, try a variety of hot and cold hors d'oeuvres. A summer soirée might include Watermelon, Manchego, and Serrano Ham Skewers (page 54), Lobster Rolls with Bacon, Tomato, and Caper Mayonnaise (page 65), and Mini Burgers with Smoked Tomato Chutney (page 69). An autumn gathering could feature Savory Apple, Cheddar, and Thyme Turnovers (page 104), Sweet Potato Cakes with Smoked Trout and Herbed Crème Fraîche (page 103), and Oysters on the Half Shell with Apple-Horseradish Slaw (page 96). Arrange the dishes on a buffet or sideboard so that guests can help themselves, giving you time to mingle or tend to other things. Or, pass the items on pretty platters, which allows you to interact with each of your guests individually.

multicourse meal If your appetizer needs consist of an initial dish to begin a larger meal, consider a seasonal soup or salad to help kick off the evening. Cold Pea Soup with Crème Fraîche and Chives (page 30) is a welcome spring starter, while a first course featuring Warm Wild Mushroom Salad with Bacon Vinaigrette (page 108) is a perfect choice in the fall.

tapas party A tradition in Spain, and a popular way of entertaining today, consider offering several small plates, meant for sharing, in lieu of a formal meal. A winter party could include Filo Rolls with Arugula, Spinach, and Feta (page 113), Crab-Stuffed Piquillo Peppers (page 118), Lobster, Avocado, and Grapefruit Cocktail (page 126), Spiced Lamb Meatballs with Garlicky Yogurt Sauce (page 121), and Truffled Fonduta with Winter Vegetables (page 134). Round out the meal with a purchased dessert.

Your appetizers should always complement the other items on your menu. Try to vary the colors, flavors, and textures to keep your guests interested. If you are serving hors d'oeuvres as prelude to a dinner party, try to avoid duplicating ingredients used in the main part of the menu. Or, consider grouping the items according to a theme. For example, a summer pan-Asian hors d'oeuvres party could include Cucumber and Avocado Summer Rolls with Mustard Soy Sauce (page 49), Grilled Chicken Skewers with Peanut-Ginger Sauce (page 62), and Lettuce Tacos with Grilled Sesame Beef (page 77).

planning your time

When including an appetizer as part of your menu, it's important to consider the complexity of the rest of the menu items as well as the serving temperatures of the dishes. Hot appetizers will need last-minute cooking and plating. Cold appetizers and dips are easy to make ahead. Be sure to plan your time wisely.

If you do not wish to be cooking after the guests have arrived, choose recipes that can be made ahead. For example, Olives and Feta Marinated with Lemon and Ouzo (page 18) can be made up to one week in advance. Chilled Poached Shrimp with Zesty Balsamic Dipping Sauce (page 33) is even better when refrigerated for up to six hours to blend the flavors. Dates Stuffed with Chorizo and Goat Cheese (page 88) take just minutes to put together and require no cooking.

For a more casual party, friends and family could gather in the kitchen and watch—or even help—while you are preparing the dishes. For example, guests could help coat the Cheese-Stuffed Risotto Cakes (page 82) in the flour, egg, and bread crumbs while you pan-fry them in batches. The rice cakes can then be consumed warm and delicious right in the kitchen while the next batch is in progress. Another idea is to have helpers roll out and top the dough rounds for Whole-Wheat Pizzette with Lamb, Broccoli Rabe, and

Olives (page 125), which then take just ten minutes to bake.

estimating quantities

The number of appetizers to include in an event depends on what type of event it is. A dinner party might feature both a finger food that is consumed right when people arrive as well as a first course when they sit down, or only one of these options. If you are serving hors d'oeuvres to precede a dinner, four or five bites per person are sufficient to spark your guests' appetites, but not suppress them for the meal that follows.

An appetizers-only party with drinks requires a bit more thought. Plan on eight to ten bites per person for every 1 to 1½ hours of party time. For a party of eight to twenty guests at which only appetizers will be served, plan on serving five or six different finger foods. A meal composed of small plates might feature five or six different selections, as well as a dessert, but make the portions slightly bigger, as they will stand in for a meal.

beverage quantities To calculate the number of beverages you will need for your party, use the following guidelines: For every two or three wine drinkers, plan on one bottle of wine. For every ten to twelve liquor drinkers, plan on one liter of liquor. For every two guests, plan to serve one liter of bottled still or sparkling water or other nonalcoholic beverage.

serving appetizers

serving vessels If you are serving appetizers as a first course or as small plates, your everyday dinnerware should work just fine for presenting them. But if you like to serve bite-sized finger foods often, it's a good idea to assemble a collection of flat round or oval platters in white or another neutral color. Remember to provide an ample supply of cocktail napkins—fabric or good-quality paper napkins—especially when you are serving messy or oily items such as Deviled Eggs with Watercress (page 24), Sweet Corn Fritters with Smoky Honey Dipping Sauce (page 61), or Curried Butternut Squash Samosas with Tamarind Chutney (page 92). Don't forget to set out an attractive vessel in which to deposit discarded items— toothpicks, shellfish shells, soiled napkins— on a nearby buffet or sideboard.

chilling and warming plates Cold appetizers are best served on chilled dishware. Be sure to put a stack of plates or bowls in the refrigerator for at least fifteen minutes before serving a cold soup, salad, or another item that's at its best when cold. In a pinch, you can put warm dishes in the freezer for a few minutes to cool them quickly. Hot foods, on the other hand, are often best when served on warmed plates or platters. To warm plates, place them in a 200°F oven for about 15 minutes.

homemade mayonnaise

2 tablespoons fresh lemon juice
1 large egg
1 large egg yolk
¼ teaspoon kosher salt
½ teaspoon dry mustard
¾ cup canola oil
¾ cup extra-virgin olive oil

In a blender, combine the lemon juice, egg, egg yolk, salt, and mustard and process on low speed for 15 seconds. With the blender running, add the canola oil, a few drops at a time, until the mixture begins to thicken. Then, add the remaining canola and the olive oil in a thin, steady stream and process continuously until the mixture becomes thick and opaque in color, 1–2 minutes. Transfer the mayonnaise to a small bowl, cover tightly, and refrigerate. Use within 4 days. Makes about 1¾ cups.

tamarind chutney

½ teaspoon ground cumin
½ teaspoon garam masala
½ teaspoon ground ginger
¼ cup seedless tamarind paste
sea salt
sugar

In a small, dry saucepan over medium heat, toast the cumin, garam masala, and ginger, shaking the pan occasionally, until fragrant, about 1 minute. Remove from the heat and let cool for about 2 minutes.

Break up the tamarind paste with your fingers and remove any extraneous seeds. Add the tamarind and 2 cups water to the pan and return to medium heat. Simmer the mixture, stirring and mashing the tamarind constantly, until reduced by one-half, about 15 minutes. Taste and adjust the seasonings with salt and sugar. Pour the chutney into a small bowl, let cool, cover, and set aside at room temperature. Makes about 1 cup.

crème fraîche

1 cup heavy cream
1 tablespoon buttermilk

In a small saucepan over medium-low heat, combine the cream and buttermilk. Heat just until the mixture is lukewarm (do not allow the mixture to simmer). Transfer the mixture to a bowl, cover, and let stand at warm room temperature until thickened, at least 8 and up to 48 hours.

Refrigerate until well chilled before using. Makes about 1 cup.

cumin-crusted pita chips

1 teaspoon cumin seeds
¾ teaspoon kosher salt
3 pita breads, 7 inches in diameter
1½ tablespoons olive oil

Preheat oven to 400°F. Line a rimmed baking sheet with aluminum foil. Toast the cumin in a small heavy frying pan over medium heat

until fragrant, about 2 minutes. Pour onto a plate to cool, then crush in a spice mill or with a mortar and pestle along with the salt, until the mixture is finely ground.

Brush the pita breads on both sides with the oil, cut them into 8 wedges each, and arrange the wedges on the prepared baking sheet. Sprinkle the tops evenly with the salt and cumin mixture. Bake until the wedges are light golden brown and crisp, 10–15 minutes, turning them over halfway through baking. Serve the pita chips warm or at room temperature. Makes 24 chips.

cornmeal tartlet dough

1 cup all-purpose flour
¼ cup stone-ground yellow cornmeal
½ teaspoon sugar
½ teaspoon kosher salt
4 tablespoons cold unsalted butter
¼ cup ice water

In a food processor, combine the flour, cornmeal, sugar, and kosher salt and pulse a few times to blend. Cut the butter into cubes, scatter over the flour mixture, and process until the mixture resembles coarse meal. With the motor running, add the ice water in a slow, steady stream and process just the dough comes together in a shaggy mass.

Remove the dough from the food processor, divide it in half, and shape each half into a thin disk. Wrap each disk separately in plastic wrap and refrigerate for at least 30 minutes to firm. Makes enough dough for 24 miniature tartlets.

whole-wheat pizza dough

2¼ cups unbleached all-purpose flour

1⅓ cups whole-wheat flour

2¼ teaspoons (1 packet) rapid-rise yeast

2 teaspoons salt

1 teaspoon sugar

1¼ cups warm water (110°F)

2 tablespoons olive oil

In a food processor, combine the all-purpose and whole-wheat flours, yeast, salt, and sugar, and pulse briefly. With the motor running, add the water and oil in a steady stream and pulse until the dough comes together in a rough mass, adding more water 1 teaspoon at a time if needed. Process for 30 seconds longer to knead the dough.

Transfer the dough to a lightly floured surface and shape it into a ball. Coat a large bowl with olive oil, then add the dough and turn it around to lightly coat it with oil. Cover with a clean kitchen towel and let rise in a warm place until doubled in bulk and very spongy, about 1½ hours.

Punch down the dough, transfer it to a lightly floured surface, and knead it into a smooth cylinder. Divide the dough into 2 equal pieces and knead again to form 2 smooth balls, adding a little flour if the dough is sticky. Cover with

the towel and let rest for 10 minutes. Makes 2 dough balls.

basic risotto

3 cups low-sodium chicken broth

2 tablespoons unsalted butter

2 tablespoons minced yellow onion

1 cup arborio rice

½ cup dry white wine

In a saucepan over high heat, bring the broth to a simmer. Reduce the heat to very low and keep the broth hot.

In a heavy saucepan over medium heat, melt the butter. When the butter has melted, add the onion and cook, stirring often, until translucent, about 3 minutes. Add the rice and stir until the kernels are well covered with the butter and are opaque, about 3 minutes. Add the wine and cook, stirring, until it is absorbed, about 2 minutes.

Ladle in about ½ cup of the hot broth, adjust the heat so the liquid bubbles gently, and stir until the broth is absorbed. Continue adding the hot broth, ½ cup at a time, and allowing it to be fully absorbed before adding more, until the rice is creamy and the kernels are just tender but still slightly firm at the center, 18–20 minutes total. If you have used all of the broth before the rice is ready, use hot water. If using for Cheese-Stuffed Risotto Cakes (page 82), let cool completely before chilling. Makes 2½ cups.

working with avocados

1 *Cut the avocado in half* Using a chef's knife, cut the avocado in half lengthwise, cutting down to and around the pit.

2 *Separate the halves* Hold the avocado so one of the halves rests in each hand. Gently rotate the halves in opposite directions to separate them.

3 *Remove the pit* Carefully holding the half with the pit in one hand, strike the pit with the heel of the knife blade, lodging it in the pit. Twist the knife and lift out the pit.

4 *Peel the avocado* Cut each avocado half in half again to make quarters. Pull the peel away from the flesh. (Alternatively, using a paring knife, cut the flesh in a grid pattern just down to the peel. Use a spoon to scoop out the avocado squares from the shell.)

working with leeks

1 *Trim the leeks* Using a chef's knife, trim off the roots and tough dark green tops of the leeks, leaving only the white and pale green parts. If the outer layer is wilted or discolored, peel it away and discard.

2 *Quarter the leeks* Cut each leek in half lengthwise. Place each half, cut side down, and cut it in half again to create quarters.

3 *Rinse the leeks* Holding the root end of the leek, and separating the layers to expose any

sand or dirt, swish the leeks in a bowl of cold water or rinse them thoroughly under cold running water.

dicing tomatoes

1 Cut lengthwise slices Use a chef's knife to make a shallow circular cut to remove the cores, if necessary. Place each tomato half cut side down on a cutting board and make a series of slices ¼ inch apart.

2 Cut the slices into strips Stack 2 or 3 of the tomato slices at a time on their sides. Make a second series of slices ¼ inch apart, perpendicular to the first. You will end up with strips.

3 Cut the strips into dice Line up the strips and cut crosswise into ¼ inch dice. Repeat steps 1–3 with the remaining tomato half.

working with citrus

Citrus fruits add bright flavor that works well with many other appetizer components. Here are some techniques for working with citrus.

zesting If a recipe calls for both citrus zest and juice, zest the fruit before juicing because the fruit is easier to zest when it is whole. To grate citrus zest, use a fine-toothed rasp-style grater. Using light pressure, move the citrus back and forth against the grater's teeth, removing only the colored rind and leaving the whitish pith on the fruit.

juicing To get the most juice from a citrus fruit, bring the fruit to room temperature and roll it back and forth along a work surface under the palm of your hand, applying firm pressure, so that the fruit softens slightly. Cut the fruit in half and use a citrus press or reamer to juice each half. Strain the juice to remove seeds or bits of pulp.

skinning and cutting

1 Cut off the top and bottom Slice off the top and bottom of the fruit, then set the fruit on one of the cut sides.

2 Remove the skin Using a sharp, thin-bladed knife, cut away the skin and white pith in strips, following the rounded contour of the fruit. Work your way around the fruit, rotating it as needed.

3 Slice the fruit, if desired If you need slices for the recipe, cut the fruit crosswise.

4 Or, cut the segments free If your recipe calls for citrus segments, hold the skinned fruit in one hand. Working over a bowl to catch the juice and segments, cut along each side of the membrane that separates the segments and let each segment drop into the bowl.

working with watermelon

1 Trim the ends Using a large chef's knife, carefully cut a slice off the top and bottom ends of the melon. Stand it on one of its flat ends on the cutting board.

2 Cut off the rind Following the curve of the fruit, cut away the peel in long strokes around the circumference of the fruit.

3 Cut the melon into strips Cut the fruit in half lengthwise, then cut each half in half again to make quarters. One at a time, lay the quarters on their sides and cut them lengthwise into even strips.

4 Cut the strips into cubes On the cutting board, line up 2 or 3 strips at a time and then cut them crosswise into rough cubes.

working with herbs

cilantro, dill, mint, parsley Pull off the leaves from the stems. Gather the leaves on a cutting board and then rock a chef's knife back and forth over the leaves to chop them coarsely. Regather the leaves and rock the blade over them until chopped into small, even pieces (finely chop) or into pieces as fine as possible (mince).

thyme Gently run your thumb and index finger down the stems to remove the petal-like leaves. Gather the leaves on a cutting board. Rock a chef's knife back and forth over the leaves to chop them coarsely. Regather the leaves and rock the blade over them until chopped into small, even pieces (finely chop) or into pieces as fine as possible (mince).

chives Gather the chives into a small bundle and place on a cutting board. Use a very sharp chef's knife to cut the chives crosswise into small pieces. Alternatively, hold the bundle in one hand and use kitchen scissors to finely snip the chives into small pieces.

pitting olives

1 Pound the olives Place the olives in a locking plastic bag, force out the air, and seal closed. Using a meat pounder or rolling pin, gently pound the olives to split the flesh. (Alternatively, press on the olives individually with the flat side of a chef's knife.)

2 Remove the pits Remove the crushed olives from the bag and separate the pits from the olive flesh with your fingers. Use a paring knife to cut the flesh from the pits of any stubborn olives.

skinning hazelnuts

1 Toast the nuts Place the nuts on a rimmed baking sheet and toast in a 350°F oven until the color deepens and they become fragrant, 15–20 minutes.

2 Rub off the skins After the nuts have cooled, rub them firmly with a kitchen towel and use your fingers to pull away any stubborn skins. If the skins don't come off easily, toast for a few minutes, then try again.

cleaning squid

1 Cut off the tentacles Using a chef's knife, cut off the tentacles just below the eyes of the squid. Be careful not to cut too far away from the eyes or the tentacles will fall apart.

2 Remove the beak Squeeze the cut end of the tentacles to expose the hard, round "beak" at the base. Pull out and discard the beak. Set the tentacles aside.

3 Remove the head and innards Gently squeeze the tubelike body, and then pull away the head. The entrails, including the ink sac, should come away with the head. Discard the head and entrails.

4 Remove the quill Reach into the body and pull out the long, transparent, plasticlike quill along with any remaining entrails and discard them. Rinse the body and tentacles under cold running water.

5 Remove the skin, if desired If you wish, pull off the dark, pinkish skin from the squid body, using a paring knife to help scrape the skin away if necessary.

6 Cut the body into rings Using a chef's knife, cut the body crosswise into rings, rinse well, and drain. Pat dry with paper towels.

rolling out pastry dough

1 Enclose the dough in waxed paper Place the dough between 2 sheets of waxed paper. Give the dough several whacks with a rolling pin to flatten and soften it a bit.

2 Roll out the dough Starting with the pin ¼ inch from one edge, begin rolling, pushing outward smoothly and stopping ¼ inch from the other edge.

3 Lift, rotate, and flip the dough Lift the dough, rotate it a quarter turn, and repeat rolling, again starting at the edge. Flip the dough over from time to time to ensure it rolls out evenly.

direct-heat grilling

charcoal grill Using long-handled tongs, arrange ignited coals into 3 heat zones: one 2 or 3 layers deep in one-third of the fire bed, another that's 1 or 2 layers deep in another third of the fire bed, leaving the final third of the fire bed free of coals. When the coals are covered with a layer of white ash, place the food on the grill grate directly over the first layer of coals, which should be the hottest. Move the food to another third of the grill if the heat seems too high, the food appears to be cooking too fast, or if flare-ups occur.

gas grill Turn on all the heat elements as high as they will go. Close the grill cover and let the grill heat for 10–20 minutes before using. When you're ready to cook, turn one of the heat elements off. Place the food on the grill grate directly over the hottest part of the grill. Turn down the heat as needed to adjust the grill temperature, or move the food to the cool zone if flare-ups occur.

seasonal ingredients

All produce has a peak season, sometimes even just a month, when the flavor is at its best. Some fish and shellfish, too, have a season during which they are plentiful and flavorful. The following chart shows the season or seasons during which a variety of foods are plentiful in the market, and at their peak of flavor.

INGREDIENTS	SPRING	SUMMER	FALL	WINTER
apples			●	○
artichokes	●		●	
arugula	●		●	●
asparagus	●			
bell peppers		●	●	
blood oranges				●
broccoli		●	●	●
broccoli rabe		●	●	●
butternut squash			●	●
cauliflower		●	●	●
chiles		●	●	
corn		●		
cucumber		●		
dungeness crab				●
eggplant		●	●	
escarole			●	●
fava beans	●			
fennel	●	●	●	●
figs		●	●	

INGREDIENTS	SPRING	SUMMER	FALL	WINTER
frisée			●	●
grapefruit	○			●
horseradish root			●	●
kale	○		●	●
leeks	●	○	●	●
lobster		●		●
meyer lemons	○			●
oysters			●	●
peas	●	○		
persimmons			●	●
pomegranates			●	●
radishes	●	●	●	
spinach	●	●	●	●
radicchio		●	●	●
sweet potatoes			●	●
tomatoes		●	○	
watercress	●			
wild mushrooms			●	●
wild salmon		●		

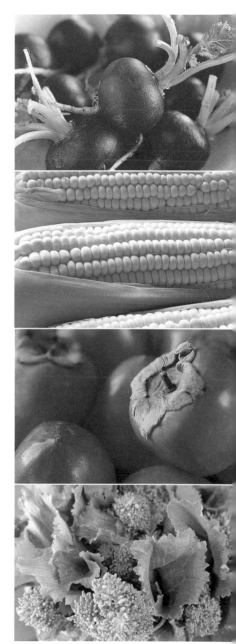

glossary

ahi tuna Also known as yellowfin tuna, ahi has a dark red flesh and meaty flavor and texture. It is delicious raw and lightly cooked, but if you're eating it this way, be sure to buy sushi- or sashimi-grade tuna.

allspice The berry of an evergreen tree, allspice tastes like a combination of cinnamon, nutmeg, and cloves. It is often used in Jamaican and Caribbean dishes, as well as in many other sweet and savory recipes.

anchovy paste Available in tubes, anchovy paste is made from ground anchovy fillets, vinegar, salt, and sugar. It is used in small amounts to bring unmatched flavor to a variety of dishes.

arugula The leaves of this dark green plant, also called rocket, resemble deeply notched, elongated oak leaves. They have a nutty, tangy, and slightly peppery flavor. The larger leaves may be more pungent than small ones.

avocado, Hass Rich in flavor and silky in texture, avocados are a favorite subtropical fruit. Almost-black Hass avocados are especially prized for their buttery flesh. For more on preparing avocados, see page 145.

bacon Cut from the belly of the hog below the spareribs, bacon is cured and usually smoked. Look for high-quality, thick-sliced bacon for the best flavor.

applewood smoked Smoked over aromatic apple wood chips, this bacon has a unique full flavor and aroma.

Berkshire Made from a heritage breed of hogs, Berkshire bacon has a fuller flavor than that of standard bacon and is cured without the use of nitrates.

beans, cannellini These ivory-colored beans possess a creamy, fluffy texture when cooked. White kidney beans or Great Northern beans can be substituted if canned cannellini beans are unavailable.

bread

country-style This general category includes any rustic, full-bodied, usually free-form yeast bread. French bread and baguettes are included in this group.

pita A flat, round bread from the Middle East made with white or wheat flour and very little leavening. Known also as pocket bread or pita pockets, the bread forms a large hollow at the center as it bakes.

broccoli rabe Also known as broccoli raab, rape, and rapini, this bright green vegetable resembles broccoli, but has slender stalks, small florets, and lots of frilly leaves. Its flavor is assertively bitter.

buttermilk In earlier times, buttermilk was the milky liquid that remained after cream was churned into butter. Today, it is made by adding a bacterial culture to milk, giving it a tangy flavor and thick texture.

capers Flower buds from a shrub native to the Mediterranean, capers are usually sold pickled in a vinegar brine. Those labeled "nonpareils," from the south of France, are the smallest and considered the best.

cayenne pepper A very hot red pepper made from ground dried cayenne and other chiles, cayenne is used sparingly to add heat or to heighten flavor. Because different blends vary in heat, always begin with a very small amount and add more to taste.

cheese Visit a cheesemonger with a rapid turnover for the best quality. Before buying, always ask to sample a piece.

cabra al vino This aged goat cheese boasts a semi-firm, creamy texture and mild flavor. It is soaked in wine for several hours, lending a fruity, slightly sweet taste, and giving its rind a vivid purple color.

farmhouse Cheddar A cow's milk cheese with a sharp, salty flavor, farmhouse Cheddars are stronger tasting than other American Cheddars.

Greek feta A young cheese made from sheep's milk, Greek feta has a crumbly texture. It comes packed in brine, which lends a pleasant, salty flavor.

fontina val d'Aosta A rich, semifirm cow's milk cheese with an earthy, mild flavor, this cheese hails from Italy's Piedmont region. Non-Italian versions of the cheese can be lacking in flavor.

goat Also called chèvre, this pure white cheese is made from goat's milk. It has a soft texture and a pleasantly tangy, slightly salty flavor. Do not used aged goat cheese in a recipe calling for fresh. See also *cabra al vino*.

Gorgonzola Italy's famous blue cheese, Gorgonzola is made from cow's milk. When young, it is creamy, soft, and mildly pungent. This version is usually labeled "dolcelatte" or "dolce." Older, riper Gorgonzola is much stronger in flavor and is labeled "piccante."

Parmigiano-Reggiano True Parmesan that comes from the Emilia-Romagna region of northern Italy. Rich and complex in flavor, it often possesses a pleasant granular texture.

pecorino romano Made from sheep's milk, pecorino is produced in nearly every region of central and southern Italy. Pecorino romano, made in the area around Rome, tends to be well aged and sharp.

ricotta Italian for "recooked," ricotta was originally made from cooking the whey drained from mozzarella cheese. It is a moist, fresh cheese with tiny curds, easily found at supermarkets, but a more flavorful version, made without stabilizers or preservatives, can be found at Italian delicatessens and artisanal cheese shops.

Manchego A Spanish sheep's milk cheese with a mild, pale yellow interior dotted with holes. It is mild tasting and pleasantly salty.

smoked mozzarella Mozzarella cheese, made from cow's milk, which has been smoked over wood smoke to lend it a pronounced smoky flavor.

chickpeas Also known as garbanzo beans or ceci beans, these large beige beans boast a firm texture and rich, nutty flavor.

chipotle chile Chipotle chiles are ripe red jalapeños that have been dried and smoked. They are widely available packed in adobo sauce, a tangy blend of tomato and onion.

chorizo, Spanish A sausage made from pork, chile and garlic, which is usually smoked. Do not substitute the Mexican version of chorizo, which is a highly spiced fresh sausage. Be sure to remove the casings from Spanish chorizo before using.

coconut milk Sold in cans, coconut milk is made by processing grated coconut and water. Before use, shake the can or stir the contents well to combine the dense cream that settles on the top with the liquid on the bottom.

cornmeal Made from yellow, white, or blue corn, cornmeal can be ground fine, medium or coarse. Stone-ground cornmeal contains the germ of the corn, giving it a fuller, slightly nutty flavor and more nutrients.

crab, Dungeness Large and delicious, the Dungeness is native to the waters of the West Coast of the United States. It can be found live in tanks, or already cooked, in fish markets and natural foods stores.

crème fraîche In the French tradition, crème fraîche is unpasteurized cream thickened by bacteria that is naturally present in the cream. More commonly, though, it is cream thickened by a bacteria that is added, yielding a soft, spreadable consistency and a tangy, slightly nutty flavor. Crème fraîche is sold in tubs in well-stocked markets, often in the specialty cheese case.

cucumber, English Slender, dark green English cucumbers, also called hothouse cucumbers, have thin skins and very few seeds. They are often sold shrink-wrapped beside regular cucumbers.

curry paste, red Popular in Thai cooking, red curry paste is a blend of red chiles, garlic, lemon grass, cilantro, kaffir lime zest, and other flavorings. It can be used to flavor a variety of dishes, from stir-fries, to stews, to dipping sauces.

curry powder, madras Curry powder is a convenience product meant to simplify the daily chore of blending spices for Indian cooks. It is a complex mixture of ground chiles, spices, seeds, and herbs. Madras curry has more heat than standard curry powder.

dates, deglet noor These dates are considered "semi-dry," meaning they have a low moisture content and firm texture. They are sold in natural food stores packed in moisture-proof packages on the store shelves, rather than in the refrigerated section.

duck, roast, Chinese-style Duck is a popular ingredient in Chinese cuisine, so much so that you often see rows of roasted birds hanging from hooks in Chinese take-out restaurants. They are perfect for using in stir-fries or as part of an appetizer featuring steamed buns or thin pancakes paired with a flavorful sauce. The meat, darker in color and fuller in flavor than chicken, and the flavorful, crisp skin, are both delicious.

escarole The robust, slightly curled leaves of this chicory relative are slightly bitter, but pleasantly so. Delicious raw, the sturdy leaves of escarole can also stand up to light cooking or warm dressings.

fava beans Also called broad beans, these springtime beans have an earthy, slightly bitter flavor. The edible portion must be removed from the large outer pod, and then each bean must be slipped out of its tough skin.

fennel Similar in appearance to celery, but with a large bulb on the end from which slimmer stems emerge, fennel has a faint licorice flavor and a crisp texture. The feathery fronds can be chopped and added to a dish as a seasoning or garnish.

figs, mission Small, dark purple, and sweet, Mission figs are also called Black Mission and California black. Figs are available twice a year, a small harvest in the summer large one in the fall, but the autumn fruits are typically larger and more flavorful. Because they do not ripen off the tree, figs must be picked ripe and are quite fragile.

filo dough Filo is a paper-thin pastry of Greek origin. It is available in the freezer section of many well-stocked food stores and in Greek and Middle Eastern markets. For the best results, let the pastry thaw very slowly, in the refrigerator if time allows. When working with filo, be sure to keep the unused sheets covered with a barely damp kitchen towel to prevent them from drying out and becoming brittle.

fish sauce Made from salted and fermented fish, fish sauce is a thin, clear liquid that ranges in color from amber to dark brown. Southeast Asians use it in the same way Westerners use salt, both as a cooking seasoning and at the table.

five-spice powder, Chinese This aromatic blend of five spices includes cinnamon, cloves, star anise, Sichuan peppercorns, and fennel or anise seeds. In some versions, ground ginger takes the place of one of the other spices.

flour Specialty flour can add exciting flavor and texture to dishes.

buckwheat Buckwheat makes a dark flour with a nutty, slightly sweet flavor and firm texture. Buckwheat flour can be found in natural foods stores.

semolina Ground from durum wheat, which is especially high in protein, semolina is used primarily for making dried pasta. It also adds an interesting, nutty flavor to breads and batters. Look for semolina flour in specialty food stores or Italian groceries.

sweet rice Ground from "sweet" rice, also called short-grain rice, sweet rice flour lends a chewy or crisp texture to recipes, depending on how it is used. Look for it in Asian markets or well-stocked supermarkets.

french, to To French, or frenching, means to cut meat away from the top of a chop or rib to expose part of a bone. Lamb chops are often found already "frenched," which gives them a cleaner, more elegant look.

frisée Actually young curly endive, frisée boasts lacy leaves gathered loosely, with tender, pale green outer leaves and a pale yellow to white heart. It has a pleasantly bitter flavor and crisp texture.

garam masala An Indian spice blend consisting of a variety of warm spices. Every home cook has their own special formula, but common spices include cinnamon, cloves, coriander, cumin, nutmeg, black pepper, cardamom, chiles, and others.

horseradish Native to Europe and Asia, this gnarled root has a spicy flavor that perks up sauces and side dishes. It can be found fresh but is more commonly sold bottled as "prepared" horseradish, already grated and mixed with vinegar.

julienne, to To julienne a vegetable refers to cutting it into very thin pieces, typically about ⅛ inch wide and thick by 2 inches long.

kale, Tuscan Also known as black kale and *cavolo nero,* Tuscan kale is a dark, sturdy, leafy green very similar to dinosaur kale. If Tuscan kale is not available, dinosaur or regular kale makes a fine substitute.

lamb Today's lamb is tender, full-flavored, and only slightly, but pleasantly, gamy.

grass fed This refers to lamb cut from sheep that have been allowed to roam their natural habitat and nourished with grass, as opposed to animals raised in large feed lots that have been fed grain and corn. The flavor of grass-fed lamb is clean and distinct, and much grass-fed lamb is organic.

sausage; see Merguez.

lox Similar to smoked salmon, lox has a less smoky, slightly saltier taste. The salmon is first brine cured, then cold smoked, which brings out the natural oils in the fish.

mandoline A flat, rectangular tool used for cutting foods quickly and easily, a mandoline usually comes with an assortment of blades to cut food into a variety of shapes. The advantages of using a mandoline over a knife are precision and regularity.

merguez sausage Made from lamb, merguez is a spicy fresh sausage originally from North Africa and now popular in a variety of Mediterranean cuisines. Its dark red color comes from the many red-colored spices and chiles that flavor it.

Meyer lemon Believed to be a cross between a regular lemon and a mandarin orange, Meyer lemons are thin-skinned and turn deep orangy yellow when ripe. Their fragrant juice and flesh are sweeter and less acidic than regular lemons. They also have a unique floral aroma.

mirin An important ingredient in Japanese cooking, mirin is a sweet cooking wine made by fermenting glutinous rice and sugar. The pale gold and syrupy wine adds a rich flavor and translucent sheen to sauces, dressings, and simmered dishes.

oil Whether the oil in a recipe is used as a flavoring, a cooking medium, or both, will inform what type to use in a recipe.

Asian sesame This deep amber–colored oil is pressed from toasted sesame seeds. It has a strong flavor and should be used sparingly as a seasoning in Asian-inspired dishes.

hazelnut Richly flavored, hazelnut oil is pressed from untoasted or toasted nuts and boasts a strong, nutty flavor. The best hazelnut oils come from France.

peanut Pressed from peanuts, which give it a hint of rich, nutty flavor, peanut oil is popular in Chinese cooking and for deep-frying, thanks to its high smoke point.

rice bran Made from the bran of the rice kernel, this oil's slightly nutty flavor and high smoke point make it a good choice for deep-frying.

truffle The best truffle oil is made by infusing black or white truffle pieces into mild olive oil. It is used sparingly to lend truffle's distinct, haunting flavor to dishes without the expense of buying a whole truffle.

olives The best way to become familiar with different types of olives is to try a few at a store that offers free samples.

Gaeta Brownish black and with a nutty flavor, the salt-cured Gaeta is soft and smooth.

Kalamata A popular olive variety from Greece, the Kalamata is almond shaped, purplish black, rich, and meaty. The olives are brine cured and then packed in oil or vinegar.

oranges, blood Originally from Sicily, blood oranges have distinctive red flesh and juice and a flavor reminiscent of berries. They are commonly found in the cuisine of the Mediterranean region.

ouzo A licorice-flavored liqueur from Greece, ouzo is clear in color and slightly sweet.

oysters, Atlantic Atlantic oysters have bumpy, elongated shells and a briny flavor with strong mineral hints. Although originally from East Coast waters, Atlantic oysters are now farmed all over the country.

panko From Japan, panko are delicate, crystal-shaped, dried bread crumbs that deliver an especially light, crisp texture to fried foods. Look for them in bags or boxes in specialty food stores or Asian markets.

paprika Made from ground dried red peppers and ranging from orange-red to red, paprika is a versatile spice. Both Hungary and Spain are large producers of paprika.

hot Paprika that has a hint of spiciness.

smoked From the *la Vera* region of Spain, smoked paprika or *Pimentón de la Vera* has a pronounced smoky flavor. It can be found in hot (picante), sweet (dulce), or bittersweet (agridulce) forms.

sweet The opposite of hot paprika, sweet paprika is very mild.

peas, English English peas, or garden peas as they are sometimes called, must be shelled before cooking. The shelled peas should be firm, bright green, and sweet enough to eat out of hand. Because their sugars quickly convert to starch, it is important to cook English peas as soon as possible.

persimmons, fuyu Fuyu persimmons are light orange in color, round in shape, and tangy-sweet in flavor. Do not substitute the more astringent, pointed Hachiya persimmon in recipes calling for the fuyu.

piquillo peppers Piquillos are a specialty of Northern Spain and are popular in Basque cuisine. They are hand-picked, fire-roasted, and peeled prior to being packed in water or oil in jars or cans.

pomegranate The deep red fruit has a thick, leathery skin, which, when split open, reveals an abundance of sweet-sour seeds. Unlike most fruits, it is the seeds that are consumed, not the flesh around them.

potatoes, fingerling Certain varieties of white potato are called fingerlings because of their narrow, knobby, fingerlike shape.

prosciutto di Parma This Italian ham is seasoned, salt-cured, air-dried rear leg of pork. Aged from 10 months to 2 years, prosciutto from Parma in the Italian region of Emilia-Romagna is considered the best of all prosciuttos. The process of curing Parma prosciutto is dictated by law and is overseen by a governing consortium.

radicchio A red-leafed chicory, radicchio has a bitter flavor and a tender but firm texture. Radicchio di Verona and radicchio di Treviso are the two common varieties; the former is globe shaped and the latter is narrow and tapered like Belgian endive. Radicchio can be cooked or used raw as a salad green.

rice, Arborio Arborio is a Northern Italian variety of medium-grain rice with a high surface-starch content that is perfect for making risotto.

rice paper Thin, dried translucent paper made from rice flour, water, and salt is known as rice paper, rice sheets, or spring roll wrappers. Indispensable to the Vietnamese kitchen, rice papers are distinguished by the cross-hatching that results from being dried on bamboo mats under a tropical sun.

saffron The stigma of a small crocus, which must be hand-picked and then dried, it takes several thousand flowers to yield just 1 ounce of dried saffron threads, explaining saffron's status as the most expensive spice. Luckily, a little goes a long way; just a pinch is needed to season foods with saffron's distinctive flavor and to lend a golden hue.

salmon, wild king King, or chinook, salmon is valued for its deep-colored, dense flesh. Whenever possible, choose wild salmon over farmed for its superior flavor. Its method of catching also has a less adverse impact on the environment than that of farmed salmon.

salt These salts have no additives, thus providing better flavor for your dishes.

kosher salt Kosher salt has large flakes that are easy to handle. Since it is less salty and has a superior flavor than regular table salt, it can be used more liberally.

sea salt Sea salt is created by natural evaporation and contains no additives, so its flavor is crisp, with hints of minerals.

sea scallops At about 1½ inches in diameter, sea scallops are large, meaty, and firm. Look for ivory-colored scallops rather than bright-white ones that get their color from being chemically treated.

serrano ham A dry-cured ham made in mountainous areas of Spain. Although similar to prosciutto, a side-by-side tasting would show subtle but distinct differences in flavor.

squid Known in Italy as calamari, squid has a mild, sweet flavor. Because squid can become tough when overheated, it is generally cooked only briefly.

tahini, roasted Also called sesame paste, tahini is made from ground sesame seeds. It has a rich, creamy texture and a concentrated sesame taste.

tamarind The fruit of a tropical tree, tamarind's long, dark pods are filled with small seeds and a distinct sweet-and-sour pulp. Tamarind is available in many forms, including blocks of tamarind paste. Look for tamarind products in specialty food stores or Latin or Asian markets.

vinegar Each type of vinegar has a unique flavor profile that makes it particularly suited for certain uses.

balsamic A slightly sweet taste and a dark caramel color characterize balsamic vinegar. Made from the must of Trebbiano grapes, balsamic vinegars are carefully barreled and aged, sometimes for decades. Aged balsamic vinegar is used in small quantities as a prized condiment. A young balsamic is a pantry staple and can be used more liberally.

champagne White wine vinegar made with Champagne grapes is lighter and milder than most white wine vinegars.

cider Made from apples, cider vinegar is noted for its distinctive apple flavor.

rice Rice vinegar is a clear, mild, and slightly sweet vinegar produced from fermented rice. It is available plain or sweetened; the latter is marketed as seasoned rice vinegar.

red wine Sharply acidic, red wine vinegar is produced when red wine is fermented for a second time.

sherry Of Spanish origin, sherry vinegar has a nutty taste and mild acidity.

wasabi A Japanese root similar to horseradish, wasabi is widely available as a dry powder or a paste and can be used to flavor a variety of dishes or dipping sauces. It has a powerful spicy kick and a pale green color.

wonton wrappers Also called wonton skins, these thin, square, pastalike sheets are available fresh in the produce section of grocery stores and in Asian markets.

yeast, rapid-rise This specially treated version of active dry yeast generally cuts the rising time of breads and batters in half. Also called quick-rise yeast, it does not need to be dissolved separately.

index

156

OXMOOR HOUSE

Oxmoor House books are distributed by Sunset Books
80 Willow Road, Menlo Park, CA 94025
Telephone: 650 324 1532
VP and Associate Publisher Jim Childs
Director of Marketing Sydney Webber
Oxmoor House and Sunset Books are divisions
of Southern Progress Corporation

WILLIAMS-SONOMA, INC.
Founder & Vice-Chairman Chuck Williams

WILLIAMS-SONOMA NEW FLAVORS SERIES
Conceived and produced by Weldon Owen Inc.
415 Jackson Street, Suite 200, San Francisco, CA 94111
Telephone: 415 291 0100 Fax: 415 291 8841
www.weldonowen.com

In Collaboration with Williams-Sonoma, Inc.
3250 Van Ness Avenue, San Francisco, CA 94109

A WELDON OWEN PRODUCTION
Copyright © 2008 Weldon Owen Inc. and Williams-Sonoma, Inc.
All rights reserved, including the right of reproduction
in whole or in part in any form.

First printed in 2008
Printed in Singapore

10 9 8 7 6 5 4 3 2 1
Library of Congress Cataloging-in-Publication Data is available.

ISBN-13: 978-0-8487-3257-8
ISBN-10: 0-8487-3257-X

This book is printed with paper harvested from well-managed forests
utilizing sustainable and environmentally sound practices.

WELDON OWEN INC.
Executive Chairman, Weldon Owen Group John Owen
CEO and President Terry Newell
VP, Sales and New Business Development Amy Kaneko
Senior VP, International Sales Stuart Laurence
Director of Finance Mark Perrigo

VP and Publisher Hannah Rahill
Executive Editor Jennifer Newens
Senior Editor Dawn Yanagihara
Associate Editor Julia Humes

VP and Creative Director Gaye Allen
Art Director Kara Church
Senior Designer Ashley Martinez
Designer Stephanie Tang
Photo Manager Meghan Hildebrand

Production Director Chris Hemesath
Production Manager Michelle Duggan
Color Manager Teri Bell

Photographer Tucker + Hossler
Food Stylist Erin Quon
Prop Stylist Leigh Noe

Additional Photography Kate Sears: pages 18, 92, 106, 123; Jean-Blaise Hall:
page 117; Shutterstock: Dennis Debono, pages 14–15; Getty Images: Ray
Kachatorian, pages 46–47, Altrendo Images, pages 110–111; Jupiter Images:
Juan Silva, page 78–79, Paul Poplis, page 139.

ACKNOWLEDGMENTS
Weldon Owen wishes to thank the following individuals for their kind
assistance: Food Stylist Assistants Jeffrey Larsen and Victoria Woollard, Photo
Consultant Andrea Stephany; Copy editor Sharon Silva; Proofreaders Kathryn
Shedrick and Carrie Bradley; Indexer Ken DellaPenta.

FREE PUBLIC LIBRARY UNION, NEW JERSEY

3 9549 00427 1962